BRAND MYSTICISM

CULTIVATE CREATIVITY & INTOXICATE YOUR AUDIENCE

STEVEN GRASSE

(The guy who created Hendrick's Gin, Sailor Jerry Rum, Narragansett Beer, and countless other brands even your mother knows)

and AARON GOLDFARB

ILLUSTRATED BY RON SHORT

RUNNING PRESS

PHILADELPHIA

Running Press
Hachette Book Group
1290 Avenue of the Americas, New York, NY 10104
www.runningpress.com
@Running_Press

Printed in Italy

First Edition: October 2022

Published by Running Press, an imprint of Perseus Books, LLC, a subsidiary of Hachette Book Group, Inc. The Running Press name and logo are trademarks of the Hachette Book Group.

The Hachette Speakers Bureau provides a wide range of authors for speaking events. To find out more, go to www.hachettespeakersbureau.com or call (866) 376-6591.

The publisher is not responsible for websites (or their content) that are not owned by the publisher.

Print book cover and interior design by Alex Camlin.

Library of Congress Cataloging-in-Publication Data
Names: Grasse, Steven, author. | Goldfarb, Aaron, author.
Title: Brand mysticism : cultivate creativity and intoxicate your audience
  / by Steven Grasse and Aaron Goldfarb.
Description: First edition. | Philadelphia : Running Press, 2022.
Identifiers: LCCN 2022001200 | ISBN 9780762475827 (hardcover) | ISBN
  9780762475810 (ebook)
Subjects: LCSH: Branding (Marketing) | Alcohol--Marketing.
Classification: LCC HF5415.1255 G74 2022 | DDC 658.8/27--dc23/eng/20220118
LC record available at https://lccn.loc.gov/2022001200

ISBNs: 978-0-7624-7582-7 (hardcover), 978-0-7624-7581-0 (ebook)

Elco

10 9 8 7 6 5 4 3 2 1

"In Italy, for thirty years under the Borgias, they had warfare, terror, murder and bloodshed, but they produced Michelangelo, Leonardo da Vinci and the Renaissance. In Switzerland, they had brotherly love, they had five hundred years of democracy and peace—and what did that produce? The Cuckoo Clock."

—Orson Welles, *The Third Man*

"A bottle of wine contains more philosophy than all the books in the world."

—Louis Pasteur

Contents

Caveat Emptor . . . XI

PART I · BEFORE BOOZE · · · 1

PART II · MY BOOZE LIFE · · · 41

Caveat Emptor

THIS IS NOT A BOOZE BOOK.

So if you're expecting that, you're in for a surprise.

This is not a marketing book either.

If that's what you're after, put it down and walk away.

This is not a self-help book.

That section is closer to the register.

And this is not a business book.

It's none of those yet all of them.

Today it seems that literally hundreds of books about spirits come out every year, nearly all of which are forgotten almost immediately. (I suppose the same could be said for marketing, self-help, and business books.) That's because most of them are written and designed for only a small group of "insiders" already in the know, a crowd that wants to buy the same message over and over again as long as it's in new packaging. It's a circle jerk!

If that has ever turned you off, please know that this book is not written for such a small niche.

This book is meant to appeal to literally anyone on planet Earth looking to live an interesting life, hone their creativity, spawn brands, market ideas, and inspire change in their field and then the world at large. It offers bite-size anecdotes, case studies, stories, teachings, and imagery from me, Steven Grasse, and my career in booze marketing, artfully designed by my own company, Quaker City Mercantile (QCM). You can see the actual ads, commercials, and campaigns mentioned in these pages by visiting www.brandmysticismbook.com.

My hope is that the lessons I've learned from this very specific journey are applicable to anyone aiming to transmit a stronger message and focus their output, no matter the arena.

So despite the cover, despite where they may or may not have shelved what you hold in your hands, buyer, beware: This is not a book like any you've read before.

Fig. 1 Me in My Hard-Headed Youth

IF A BONEHEAD LIKE ME CAN DO THIS...

IN THE WINTER OF 1998, one of my advertising clients, William Grant & Sons (WGS), came to me with an assignment: Create a gin brand from scratch, as their portfolio was sorely lacking one.

I wondered, why me?

At the time, I was just a simple Philadelphia ad man working with brands such as R. J. Reynolds, PUMA, MTV, and ESPN. My only alcohol client back then was WGS's Glenfiddich single malt scotch, and only the American portion of the business at that.

I was hardly in the alcohol business.

I was absolutely not a distiller.

I didn't know how gin was made.

I rarely even drank it!

In retrospect, that was probably a good thing.

A year later, we had a completely new product on the market.

You know it as Hendrick's Gin.

Hendrick's Gin is magical. It literally created the concept of craft gin. Before Hendrick's, there were a few big players that had been on the market for centuries—Beefeater, Gordon's, Tanqueray—and all were seen as the stuff old people drank. Gin your grandma kept in her dusty liquor cabinet, whipping it out on rare occasions to make a dry martini with some olives from a jar in the fridge.

Today, there are hundreds upon hundreds of gin brands across the globe, each striving to be weirder than the next. Some barely even have juniper in them.

But Hendrick's was the first, and it's still the most iconic and certainly the most beloved. In a crowded field of players, it stands out two decades later. It's pretty much impossible to walk into a drinking establishment anywhere on planet Earth and not see it placed prominently on the back bar.

I'm not exaggerating when I say it completely revolutionized the spirits industry.

Fig. 2 Please Allow Me to Introduce Myself

That happened not because I was a distiller or because I knew the alcohol business or because I particularly loved gin but because I knew how to create great, sticky brands after more than a decade of experimentation in advertising everything from cigarettes to sneakers. In this case, I simply turned my skills and creativity toward the spirits world.

And when I saw how nicely it all worked out, how artistically satisfying it was, how much more fun creating and launching Hendrick's was than anything I'd done professionally before that . . .

Well, everything in my life changed.

This is my story.

WAIT! I'VE STILL NEVER HEARD OF YOU

OKAY, YOU DON'T KNOW WHO I AM, but you probably know the alcohol brands I have created (unless you live under a rock).

The exact same week that I created Hendrick's, I also created Sailor Jerry Rum, which has likewise become one of the most ubiquitous brands in its category.

In 2008, I played a key role in reviving the dormant Narragansett beer brand, and then I started flying around the world, acting as a sort of Big Beer self-esteem coach, helping give a new lease on life to brands such as Guinness, Pilsner Urquell, and Miller High Life, the last of which has now replaced PBR as the dive bar beer du jour in many people's eyes.

If that wasn't enough, that same year I founded Art in the Age of Mechanical Reproduction, an artists collective, inspired by philosopher Walter Benjamin, that would aim to develop spirits using recipes and ingredients drawn from the folk history of Pennsylvania. In other words, products from a preindustrial era, before manufacturing turned the world to shit. Maybe you've seen Root—our liqueur based on the original recipe for root beer (which was once alcoholic!)—in some hip cocktail bar on your travels.

Since 2015, I've also owned my own distillery, Tamworth Distilling, the culmination of my life's work. It pretty much revived an entire town in New Hampshire and now creates beautiful, scratch-made, handcrafted things. This artisan distillery has become a sensation not only by producing some incredible farm-to-bottle products, such as Old Hampshire Applejack and Chocorua straight rye whiskey, but also by setting off "creative grenades" and going internationally viral for its totally madcap one-offs, such as Eau De Musc, a whiskey made from beaver anus, and Graverobber Unholy Rye, produced with maple syrup tapped from colonial-era graveside maple trees.

You might wonder how I became such a Big Cheese in the world of booze.

I sometimes wonder the same thing.

I've never been the VP of some fancy ad agency. I've never been based on Madison Avenue. (I've never even worked in New York City.) I don't have an

MBA. I didn't go to an Ivy League school either—heck I had such terrible SAT scores that I'm surprised I got into any college.

I managed to start my first ad agency, Gyro Worldwide, at twenty-three years old, working out of the top floor of my father's print shop. I didn't have rich parents (I grew up in Pennsylvania's Mennonite country, surrounded by sheep), and I never took out a bank loan. I've yet to accept any venture capital (VC) money.

Today, QCM employs eighty-three people and creates new booze brands just about every week of the year. Many of which you will one day hear of and read about and hopefully buy and quite possibly enjoy.

I look at myself and think, Here I am, against all odds, having a ball, creating amazing things, and getting PAID. Like I said, if a bonehead like me can do this, YOU CAN TOO!

In this book, I'm going to explain exactly how I did what I did. And, more importantly, how you can do what *you* want to do.

How I've learned to cultivate my curiosity over the years and use it at QCM to create, design, launch (and sometimes relaunch) some of the biggest and most iconic alcohol brands of the twenty-first century.

I'll offer some case studies and lessons to follow and tell you about some rollicking adventures I had along the way. Because living an interesting life is the absolute most important thing you can do in this world.

DISCLAIMER!

WHILE EVERYTHING YOU READ IN THIS BOOK IS TRUE, IT IS ALSO TOTAL BULLSHIT.

DISCLAIMER!

IN PART I OF THIS BOOK—"Before Booze"—I will explain how my youthful passions led me to Thailand, Nepal, and New Zealand, experiencing cultures, inhaling books, and working odd jobs while I was supposed to be trapped in a classroom in snowy Syracuse.

These adventures are really important because without them, Hendrick's, or any of the other brands that I created, never would have happened.

You see, after over three decades in the business, I've realized that original creation begins by developing a broad range of deep, esoteric knowledge and experiences.

You need to have a lot of interests. If you're just bingeing the same shows on Netflix, reading the same stuff on Twitter, sharing the same Instagram memes, and watching the same dumb TikTok dances as everyone else, then how can you possibly create something truly unique and original?

My long, strange journey is the perfect example.

This isn't a story of redemption; it's a story of transformation.

And most importantly, it's a story of enchantment.

It's the story of a precocious twentysomething ad man who doesn't understand the power within him and is mostly interested in pranking people, being talked about on the news, and making his friends and coworkers laugh. But by doing those things—by treating ad work as gonzo performance art pieces—I inadvertently discovered how to truly harness my powers when I finally did enter the booze world.

If you picked up this book because you truly care only about the takeaways, that's fine—skip to Part II. You'll still enjoy the book, but you'll get less out of it. The Part II lessons of my life occurred only because of that first decade I spent slinging cigarettes for R. J. Reynolds, dropping sneakers for PUMA, inventing a fake airline that got international press, and intentionally producing a terrible movie that vexed Hollywood.

I needed to do all those things to fully understand how to create a Hendrick's Gin, how to launch a Sailor Jerry Rum, how to make a beaver anus whiskey go viral, and how to produce so many other interesting booze brands.

Let me put up that disclaimer again.

DISCLAIMER!

WHILE EVERYTHING YOU READ IN THIS BOOK IS TRUE, IT IS ALSO TOTAL BULLSHIT.

DISCLAIMER!

Because, really, I have no idea if the exact steps I took can work for you. Any author who claims they do is full of shit. There's no magic formula. At the end of the day, we all need to find our own way. Creativity isn't simply mimicking what has worked for others.

(That's its antithesis, actually.)

Instead, I hope to teach you how to cultivate your own inspiration, mine it, and then turn it into something truly unique and interesting. I can also tell you what has worked for me and some simple rules that I live by.

To put it another way: This book is full of how-to tips, crazy adventures, and off-the-grid thinking that just might save your career and spice up your miserable existence.

Literally everything you will read in this book is counterintuitive to what they teach you in business school. As you can tell, I'm not exactly a big fan of business schools. (Although if any of them want to bulk order this book, I could find a way to start liking them.)

Think of me as the Ben Franklin of hooch, the Thomas Edison of booze. Or just think of me as a crazy middle-aged man who is going to tell you some really funny, sometimes slightly fucked-up stories that will hopefully make you laugh and maybe realize there's quite a bit of merit to having fun, trolling people, doing art for art's sake, simply trying shit, and not really giving a rat's ass.

But really, I'll say it again: You need to live an interesting life if you want to create interesting things.

Fig. 3 Hat Trick

I

BEFORE BOOZE

This is my journey, my "path to enlighten-ment" if you believe that kind of stuff. In this part of the book, I am Siddhartha sit-ting under the Bodhi Tree, meditating until I have reached enlightenment and become Buddha. I am Odysseus traveling to the Underworld, meeting my prophets and sor-ceresses before I can make it to my rightful home. ☞ A little less pretentiously put: this is all the crazy shit I had to do in my life before I could fulfill my potential in the wonderful world of alcohol.

Fig. 4 I Spy with My Little Eye . . . Commie Bastards!

AVOIDING THE KHMER ROUGE AND UNDERSTANDING THE VALUE OF OLD BOOKS

I HEARD CANNONS BOOMING ALL DAY and night from the jungle. The villagers warned me to never ride my motorcycle too far off the beaten path because I might be kidnapped by the Khmer Rouge. At the time—1982, maybe 1983—the Khmer Rouge were grabbing villagers because they needed fresh blood for transfusions for their countless wounded soldiers.

I was the very first exchange student ever sent to this tiny rural village in Chanthaburi Province in eastern Thailand, four hundred miles from Bangkok on the border with Cambodia. I was an eighteen-year-old taking a sort of gap year after high school and before college.

Really, I just wanted to get the fuck out of my podunk Pennsylvania town.

What was I thinking?

I hadn't asked to go to Chanthaburi. It was a pure spin of the roulette wheel. I had never even heard of it. I barely knew where Thailand was at the time. I went to your typically shitty American public high school, and my geography knowledge reflected that.

I was stunned when I arrived.

The area had literally no tourists. The only other Western dude I ever saw during my time there was a Peace Corps worker, but he left soon after I arrived. No one but me spoke English. The locals worked on tropical fruit plantations and in ruby mines.

I should have been miserable.

Before I got to Thailand, I had been living the All-American, John Cougar Mellencamp teenaged life: cruising the McDonald's parking lot in my GTO, going to secret keggers in the woods, dating girls.

Suddenly I was transported to a tiny village right next to an active war zone. It was so remote, so unfamiliar to a bumpkin like me. There were no TVs, no movie theaters, no fast food. When I wasn't eating squid, I was eating fish eyes or chicken feet or dried blood or some strange fruit that smelled awful to me. (Durian fruit was grown everywhere in Chanthaburi, and as you'll eventually witness, I never forgot it.)

To repeat: I should have been miserable.

But I wasn't at all.

That's because I realized early on that I would be forced to entertain myself as long as I was there.

My stint in Thailand was literally the first time I ever picked up a book.

At that aforementioned typically shitty American public high school, I had literally sailed through without ever reading a single book. *Not one.*

Now, alone in Thailand, with little else to do and a language barrier separating me from everyone I met, I was inhaling them.

Peter the Great by Robert Massie.

Siddhartha by Herman Hesse.

Junky and *Naked Lunch* by William S. Burroughs.

Breakfast of Champions by Kurt Vonnegut.

King Rat by James Clavell.

The World According to Garp by John Irving.

The Hobbit and all three volumes of *The Lord of the Rings* by J. R. R. Tolkien. (Tolkien was particularly influential; you'll soon see why.)

It was a transformative experience.

The first great pivot of my life.

Without knowing it, I had gained a thirst for cultivating my own curiosity.

I arrived in Thailand one person and would leave another. (And after all the Thai kickboxing I did, I was a lot tougher too.)

In Chanthaburi, I realized a few key things and made a few changes that would define how I would immediately start living my life.

Being alone is pretty powerful. It gives you time to think and come up with plans. As the world got crazier and crazier, this would become even more valuable to me.

Because I couldn't turn on the TV and the internet didn't yet exist, I found the patience to read long books. It's harder nowadays with all the distractions bombarding you, but I still devour books.

I learned to appreciate other cultures and experiences and not judge them. To simply enjoy them and learn from them. And to not be an annoying and loud American. (I won't guarantee I've always succeeded on that last point, as you'll see later when I end up trolling all of Britain.)

I taught myself to find poetry and beauty in the mundane and the everyday. I realized how crucial it was to always keep my head up and observe the weirdness around me. Because it's always there!

My perception of what "fun" is also changed. Instead of considering it an immediate blissed-out rush, something most Americans strive for, I started thinking more long term, more project oriented. I was now willing to plant seeds and let them grow over time.

Oddly, I also internalized a great reverence for big international brands that I had never really thought about before. I was fascinated by how the Coca-Cola and Lever Brothers and Procter & Gamble brands tailored their message for Thai culture. What was similar to what I had seen in the States, what was different—it was all fascinating to me. It was because of that, there in Thailand at age eighteen, that I realized I wanted to go into advertising as a career.

Finally one of the craziest things I noticed in Chanthaburi was that people seemed to think I knew what I was doing simply because I was an American. Just because I was so completely different from them.

Most Americans, of course, believe that they have to go to the right business school or work at the right agency—build the right *pedigree*—before they will ever be taken seriously. But in that little village in Thailand, it was as if I was famous just for not being Thai, and not like everyone else.

And that gave me the first great idea of my life.

Shit! This is how I could launch my career.

Fig. 5 Foreign Exchange for Dummies

{6}

TAKING A GLOBAL VISION QUEST,
TURNING INTO ONE ODD FELLOW

As I mentioned, it's a minor miracle that I even got into college. I scored miserably on the SATs. My combined score was only three digits; all the so-called dumb jocks on athletic scholarships at Syracuse had higher SAT scores than I did.

Still, Thailand had so changed me, had so matured me, that I flourished in my freshman year (when I wasn't stepping over vomit in the freshman dorm bathrooms from my fellow residents' binge drinking the night before). Thailand had given me my life's path, so I majored in advertising but minored in South Asian studies and took a lot of classes on Sanskrit and Hindu literature. They just interested me, stoked my curiosity.

I actually got a 4.0 my first semester, and the dean was so surprised that he called me into his office. He ended up letting me into Syracuse's prestigious Newhouse School, which was then, as now, the country's number-one-ranked school of journalism and communications.

While in Thailand, I'd come up with this whole scheme to go off to college for a year and then use Syracuse to facilitate more overseas adventures where I could build an incredible résumé and start writing the story of myself.

So, sophomore year, I got into a scholarship program that sent me to Kathmandu, Nepal, where I worked as a research scholar for Royal Tribhuvan University. While I was there, I wrote and self-published a book about how to market Apple computers in the Himalayas. No joke. It was called *Apples in High Places*. ("A case study of promotional techniques used in the Himalayan Kingdom of Nepal," it says on the cover.) I used to work in the art department of my dad's printing shop, so I knew how to set type and do page layouts. In those pre-internet days, I did a ton of sleuthing to find the names and addresses of influential people to send copies to, hoping that would get them to notice me.

Then I headed back to Thailand, this time to big-city Bangkok, for an internship at Kenyon & Eckhardt (which eventually became Bozell and is now part of some global Death Star of a company). Next I moved to Hong Kong for an internship with Ogilvy.

All this travel was teaching me to be superindependent, often in extreme circumstances. It gave me a whole different understanding of how the world works. It made me a hell of a lot ballsier too.

The first semester of junior year, I got a gig at TBWA, a top international advertising agency, in London. That summer, I was hired as an intern by Young & Rubicam, the first creative intern in their history, I was told. Their head dude personally tracked me down at Syracuse and called my dorm's community floor phone. He'd gotten hold of a copy of my Apple book and was impressed. My strategy had worked.

Somewhere in there, as I can barely recall, I went back to Syracuse for my senior year and managed to graduate.

Young & Rubicam offered me a full-time job after graduation, but I blew their minds by turning it down. John Doig, a New Zealander who was the creative director of Ogilvy in Hong Kong when I was there, had advised me on that move. He told me if I took that job, I would "rot." He told me to go instead to someplace a little wild and off the beaten path where I could fake it 'til I made it. Why not New Zealand?

Throughout my whole life, I've had such luck simply through writing letters to important people. Whatever you want to do, just write a letter, or email nowadays, to the biggest person there is. So few people bother to do that, I guess it stands out. This time, I wrote a letter to Charles and Maurice Saatchi of Saatchi & Saatchi, another top agency. It worked!

"You've got a job, kid!" they told me, and I immediately got on a plane and shipped out to their New Zealand office in Auckland. After a stint at Saatchi & Saatchi, I jumped to McCann Erickson. They were a great agency in America, but their New Zealand branch was a disaster. I quickly made the worst agency in New Zealand into one of the most creative. Within McCann's global network, I started to be known as the wunderkind.

McCann offered me a chance to be the creative director at their shop in Singapore—I would have been the youngest creative director in their entire global

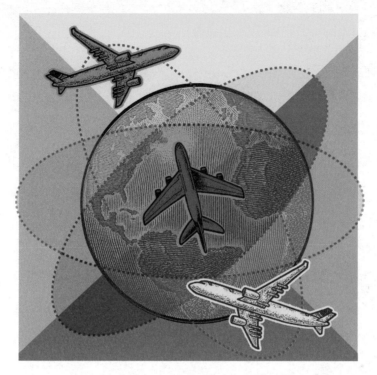

Fig. 6 Booking a Direct Flight in Pre-Internet Times

network. But I turned it down. Every expat I ran into seemed to me to be some-what sad, lonely, and lost. I also didn't want to lose track of my family back home.

So I returned to Philadelphia in 1988—with a girl, Emma, I'd met in New Zealand who would soon become my first wife—and started my first company: Gyro Worldwide.

We moved into a dust-colored former bank building on the corner of Third and Walnut in a then derelict neighborhood known as Old City. It looked as if we had acquired it from a subject on *Hoarders*: a total mess, with thumbtacked posters and dirty jokes taped to the bathroom stalls.

I was twenty-three years old.

Now I just needed some clients.

Fig. 7 Mind Blown

GOING A LITTLE INSANE, BEGINNING TO UNDERSTAND VIRALITY

WE STARTED SENDING FAXES to any local business we could think of—the Philadelphia Eagles, Urban Outfitters, the local pretzel-cart guy, you name it. We were relentless.

After reading Douglas Coupland's landmark book, *Generation X*, we got the idea to start spinning our young age and lack of experience into an advantage by labeling ourselves the official agency of Generation X. And to our astonishment, it not only worked but worked brilliantly.

Back then, before the internet changed everything, MTV was still considered cool. They even still played music videos. So, again, I wrote a letter to the biggest person there, Abby Terkuhle, their creative director at the time. I claimed our youth and *lack* of experience were actually advantages. Had he even read Douglas Coupland's *Generation X*?

As I said, I didn't have age on my side, but I did have an amazing portfolio from my days in New Zealand, and I pitched him some of my best ideas. He loved a few of them and gave me some assignments. Our first spot is, in my opinion, the epitome of Gen X marketing from this era. It was directed by Peter Care, who is probably most famous for doing many of R.E.M.'s great videos, including "Man on the Moon." It shows young twentysomethings, sometimes alone, often in twosomes, simply being themselves, staring into the camera while holding up abstract paintings created by cult artist Doug Aitken. Over them, a voiceover artist intones Samuel Ullman's poem "Youth," which begins, "Youth is not a time of life, it is a state of mind."

Terkuhle loved it, and Gyro Worldwide was soon doing on-air promos, movie award bumpers, and VMA commercials for the network. In my opinion, we would really help MTV define its '90s style of fast cuts and walls of bold, flashing colors that formed a bridge between often incongruous segments.

Now that I was a part of the Viacom network, I really wanted to get some work for something it was about to launch called Comedy Central. But Marc Chusid, the head of the channel, wouldn't give me a meeting, no matter how many crazy letters I sent him. So one morning, I decided to take matters into my own hands, hopped the train into Penn Station, and headed straight for his office.

Did I mention I was dressed as a nun?

You see, back then, Gyro Worldwide really acted like a punk rock band, like the Sex Pistols or Ramones. Like them, we thought we could best grow our profile by being outrageous. If I was our lead singer, I needed to be the most outrageous. This was before social media, and before camera phones, of course, so it was a lot harder to be outrageous and quickly go viral. As I sat there in the Comedy Central waiting room with one of my art directors, the receptionist had no idea why we were dressed like nuns, and I'm not sure we did either.

Fig. 8 How to Survive a Robot Uprising

Still, the hubbub it created forced Chusid out of his office, and he finally agreed to take that meeting with me. I walked out an hour later with an agreement to do a campaign to launch Comedy Central.

From there, our reputation continued to grow, and Gyro got jobs with HBO, Showtime, and ESPN2.

I wrote to August Busch III, then president of Budweiser, and said, "You're doing it all wrong." He hired us to do a Gen X version of a Bud Lite Spotlight and gave us half a million dollars to plan an entire road-trip promotion. This was a giant payday for us at the time.

Then I did the same for Coca-Cola. I learned it was all about having the balls to ask.

How was such a young guy getting all this high-profile work? you might wonder. Because I kept turning the negatives against me into positives.

If most companies in those days were looking at Gen X as lazy and cynical deadbeats, I knew I was the guy who could actually figure out how to market to these people who hated all forms of advertising. I was very determined.

I've always had a big chip on my shoulder. I felt that we at Gyro had something to prove. And we tried to find any way to get there, no matter how brash we had to be.

Everything we did felt like a prank on the world—anything to get attention.

We really started defining the Gyro Worldwide ethos and style when we did some print ads for Zipperhead, a kinda trashy yet totally iconic punk rock, mom-and-pop clothing store on South Street. They often had mannequins dressed in S&M gear displayed in their windows. I liked them and really wanted to work for them, but they didn't have much of a budget.

They were about to have what they dubbed a "killer" sale, and I had an idea. I told them, "Hey, I'm going to make something for you; you don't have to pay me, and we're going to get a mutual benefit out of it from all the outrage it causes."

This would be something so over-the-top crazy that I knew I wouldn't have been allowed to do it with my big-money corporate clients.

They agreed.

We made a set of dark ads that had photos of serial killers on them. They each had a tagline, stuff like "Go a little insane now, not a lot insane later—Zipperhead's Killer Sale."

Now here's the great thing: We never hung the posters anywhere in public. And they never appeared in any magazines or newspapers.

Remember, Zipperhead hadn't even hired us!

We simply sent them out to the local press. But that was enough to get millions of impressions and a ton of global coverage for Zipperhead. Some good, like a big feature in the *New York Times* Sunday Styles section, though a lot of it was hell-bent on turning Gyro into an ad world pariah.

It didn't matter to me. At this point, we really needed any press we could get.

A few of our more staid clients—big ones such as Comcast—immediately fired us for the stunt, saying we had pushed things too far. I kind of expected that. Of course, the outrage we generated landed us a ton more new clients, and more interesting ones at that. That taught me a valuable lesson.

As the Zipperhead ad with the wild-eyed visage of Charles Manson said, "Everyone has the occasional urge to go wild and do something completely outrageous. When you fight this urge it builds up within you until one day you snap."

I realized that to truly make it in this business, I should embrace my insanity, embrace the darkness of the world by turning it into art, reveling in the visceral power of violent consumerism and courting scandal. I was quickly realizing that if I didn't do that, if I continued to work for boring corporate clients, I too would eventually snap.

We even told Zipperhead to tell a pearl-clutching journalist writing a hit piece on us, "Come into the store sometime. There's something here to offend anyone."

Doing something wild and completely outrageous had allowed us to go viral, even before that term existed.

Still, I don't know how we ever got paid. All the fucked-up shit that we did got a lot more press coverage than cold, hard cash if I'm being honest.

I realized I needed to fully control, if not own, the brands I was making go viral.

That way, the buzz would also pay the bills.

RED KAMEL AND THE MARKETING MARINE CORPS

"JOE CAMEL is the best antismoking campaign of all time," I told R. J. Reynolds. "Because it sucks!"

And that was . . . *eventually* . . . how I landed the client for the first brand I ever created, Red Kamel.

By the early 1990s, I was flying into Greensboro, North Carolina, quite a bit, as we had Hanes as a client and were working on a sock brand called E. G. Smith. And every time I drove my rental car to Hanes headquarters in Winston-Salem, I passed the R. J. Reynolds Tobacco Company and saw its giant water tower looming over everything, the Camel logo like a beacon on the side.

I probably don't need to tell you that its mascot at the time, Joe Camel, looked like a giant phallus. By now everyone knows that. But back then, it wasn't really talked about.

Are they serious with that shit? I always thought.

I also thought, We should really try to work with them.

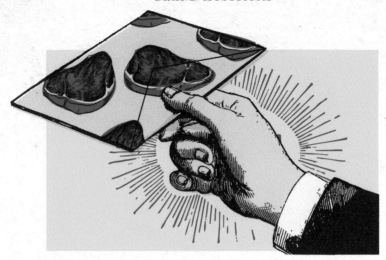

Fig. 9 Pleased to Meat You

Back then, R. J. Reynolds was making one out of every three cigarettes in the world, and it was not yet totally forbidden to try to make cigarettes interesting to the public. And even if it had been, we thought, how punk rock would it be to have a Big Tobacco client?

This was before their CEO had to testify before Congress, before the tobacco companies were sued for health care costs and forced to restrict advertising. For you young readers, this was back when you could still smoke in most bars, restaurants, and even office buildings.

So I sent the company samples of our ad work along with a handwritten letter—again, a letter!—that simply said, "Joe Camel is the best antismoking campaign of all time!"

I wrapped the package in brown kraft paper and covered it with stickers that were images of raw meat.

(Again, I have no idea why I did this. Although I do know you couldn't do that these days—you'd be treated like some kind of threat, and rightly so.)

Almost immediately, the assistant of some high-level exec called and told me to get my ass down to North Carolina. I'd obviously hit a nerve.

You see, R. J. Reynolds absolutely loved Joe Camel. The character had only been used to advertise in the United States since 1988, but the people there already thought he was iconic and the campaign clever. They were confused about why I could possibly dislike him. They truly couldn't fathom someone not loving Joe Camel.

"Okay, Mr. Smartypants, so what would you do?" their execs asked me.

Let me just state right here:

I did not really know what I was doing at that time.

I was still experimenting with my creativity, trying all sorts of different stuff to develop my aesthetic and ethos.

I asked if I could look through the company archives, and they sent me to a dark underground basement. There, while sorting through dusty old files, I discovered this brand they owned called Red Kamel. I thought it was the coolest thing ever. It was bold, mysterious, and very sexy. And they weren't using it at all!

You see, when R. J. Reynolds—the man—came out with the Camel brand in 1913, he had to buy out a similarly named brand called Red Kamel, which was based in Philadelphia. Red Kamel—with a "K"—was available only in pool halls, hotels, and, ahem, houses of "ill repute," where it was sold at a premium.

It hit me then. The key to turning around Camel wasn't in actually turning around Camel—it would be in letting me come out with my own cool-as-shit sub-brand with the Red Kamel name that would cast a halo over the main Camel brand.

And most importantly, I was certain it would get Marlboro smokers to switch over.

(The fact that Red Kamel was originally from Philadelphia also seemed like kismet.)

They absolutely hated my idea!

And sent my ass back to Philadelphia.

Oh well.

Two years later, I got a call from this guy, Brice OBrien, who was the summer intern. He told me he had found my campaign for Red Kamel in the storage closet and asked if I would be interested in coming back down to meet with him.

I did, and we decided to revive Red Kamel together.

This would be my—and Gyro's—first time creating a new product completely from scratch.

To demonstrate how fucking rich Big Tobacco was at the time, they gave me and Brice—a summer intern, mind you—an advertising budget of some ridiculous number like $25 million for the campaign. This was mere pocket change for them but a massive amount for us. Overnight, our rinky-dink Philadelphia ad agency suddenly felt as if we had Monopoly money flowing through it, and we quickly realized that we would be capable of fucking around more than ever.

I knew we couldn't simply recreate the old Red Kamel packages. That wouldn't intrigue people. Instead, we made all sorts of packages that each looked a little different and had a certain indescribable timelessness. They were a mélange of old Red Kamel images from the archives mixed with Barbarella babes, giant robots, World War II pinup girls, retrofuturist space-age lasers, and bold Soviet-era lettering (a style of font we found to be the quickest way to penetrate the consumer psyche).

This was the future as imagined by the past just as a new millennium neared. No one had ever done anything like this before that I knew of. That is, make a sort of gorgeous, transhistorical remix to sell a brand.

"Back after 80 years for no good reason except they taste good" was our new motto for Red Kamel when we relaunched it in 1996. (Imagine even implying that cigarettes taste good today! My god.)

This was a sort of antiadvertising aimed at twentysomethings who didn't want to be advertised to. We sold them mostly in hip downtown nightclubs in New York, San Francisco, and Los Angeles. Soon people who didn't live in those places were asking friends to ship them cartons. In a way, we had presaged how the whiskey business would eventually work, with collectors having friends search the globe to find limited releases for them.

Working in cigarettes, which even then were beginning to be detested by many, really taught me how to break through to people who have no interest in hearing from you. That's one reason I call my work for R. J. Reynolds the "marketing marine corps."

Being overseen essentially by only an intern meant we were free to try a whole bunch of crazy stuff that a major corporation like R. J. Reynolds normally would never let happen.

We were able to create ads that were night-and-day different from all the other boring cigarette ads out there.

Some were highly reminiscent of film noir.

For one, we had a bunch of Playboy models attacking a robot—this shit was crazy. (I think the aforementioned CEO called me a "fucking idiot" when he first saw that one.)

For another, we paid Steve McQueen's son a fortune to consult for the stunts. Just because we could.

Ultimately, *Time* named Red Kamel the best packaging of the year.

Fig. 10 Smoke 'Em If You Got 'Em

We were also the first people to ever advertise cigarettes in alt weeklies. And we never ran the same ad twice! Red Kamel literally funded some of those publications' existence for much of the '90s.

Soon big companies such as Altoids were ripping off our Red Kamel aesthetic. I was told that Liam and Noel Gallagher of Oasis, then the coolest band in the world, totally freaked out when they first saw Red Kamel. Could it even be that Shepard Fairey was inspired by our Red Kamel campaign? The red-and-yellow color palette, the bold lines, the retro iconography. Do me a favor and Google Image his *New World Odor* (2005) and *Guns and Roses* (2006) and decide for yourself. If he wasn't inspired, it's an amazing coincidence.

Clearly the campaign had really resonated with the public and really turned around Camel's fortunes. (It would lead to Brice OBrien eventually becoming the company's president of innovations.)

It had taught me that yes, you could reinvent a flagging brand with another sub-brand—something I would do a decade or more later in the Big Beer world.

It also taught me that it was probably a good idea to ignore trends and what everyone else was/is doing. Instead, open some dusty archives and dig into the past. See what worked before anyone was born and revive it in a fresh, cool way.

Eventually the tobacco industry came under the FDA's purview, where it totally should be. This meant much tighter restrictions on ads and no more Playboy models shooting laser guns or stuntmen jumping from helicopters. Hey, it was fun while it lasted. But it really shouldn't have lasted, if you know what I mean.

Still, my work on Red Kamel had allowed me to understand what I would eventually dub *brand mysticism.*

I would just need to focus on a way more socially acceptable vice.

LEARNING THE VALUE OF BEING A TROLL
AND FUCKING WITH PEOPLE

ONE OF THE UNINTENDED, unexpected perks of having a tobacco client was that they gave us so much dang money and required Gyro to have so many art directors on staff, just in case, that we had ample free time to goof around with very little fear of being fired.

There was sometimes nothing else for a lot of my employees to do *but* goof around.

So in our spare time, we amused ourselves by creating elaborate pranks and unleashing them on an unsuspecting world. I had my staff execute crazy PR stunts or create and run ads for made-up brands.

We would literally try to see how far we could push extremes of good taste and culture. Not for any legitimate reason.

But because it was a blast.

One time, we created a fake airline, Derrie-Air, to spoof the major airlines' ridiculous penny-pinching and often dehumanizing policies.

We claimed to be a carbon-neutral luxury airliner that encouraged you to "do your part." We said we had a sliding scale, and the more you weighed, the more you'd have to pay for a ticket, up to $2.25 per pound to get to Los Angeles. After all, we said, it takes more fuel, and harms the environment more, to get a heavier person from point A to point B.

It just seemed like something gross the airlines would do, and we found it funny, so that was why we did it. I didn't expect anything to come of it. It just made us laugh around the office.

Until we landed the *Philly Inquirer* as a client.

Their brief to us was to somehow prove that advertising in their newspapers was still effective. I thought, I have just the thing: Derrie-Air!

I sold them on the idea of running ads for the fake airline in both the *Inquirer* and the *Philadelphia Daily News.* They ran thirty-seven different Derrie-Air ads in both publications on a single day. And, wouldn't you know it, Derrie-Air went viral.

The Associated Press picked it up. Then every other wire service. It even got on Stephen Colbert's show!

Derrie-Air had started out as a joke, but now it was a legit hit.

So not only did it make us laugh, but it got our company a lot of attention and ultimately a lot of business. It helped the *Inquirer* get more advertisers too. (And we were sadly prescient—in early 2021, the FAA advised that airlines might want to start weighing passengers before they boarded the aircraft. Sick!)

I really think it's fun to fuck with people. Not in a cruel way, of course. Just harmless pranks that make you laugh once you find out you've been had.

We did another fake ad once in *Philadelphia Weekly*, a local alt paper that, likewise, wanted to pay us in trade. So we created a fake beer, Sphincter Boy Cream Ale. "Wrap your lips around this Sphincter—like nothing you've ever tasted before!" That caused a huge outcry. Even an edgy alt weekly said we'd gone too far.

I loved it, though. It's fun to be a smartass, and we thought we were the smartest asses back then.

It translated into real-world interactions too. When we had offices on Third and Walnut, by Independence Hall, foreign tourists frequently came in, lost and thinking our building was part of the tour. So I made fliers and created an extensive history about us being some ad agency created by George Washington in Revolutionary War times. People ate it up.

Stuff like this wasn't just fun for our employees; it kept their creative juices flowing. It kept them engaged.

And I soon realized that all these trolls were also helping me figure out how the world worked, how different industries worked, what things actually pushed people's buttons, and what things caused true outrage—and what didn't.

Even better, against all odds, the better the joke and the more effective the troll, the more likely they were to somehow end up generating income for us.

That was what happened when I decided to be a wise guy to one client who was a direct descendant of one of the UK's most notorious prime ministers. I had grown tired of him always going on and on about how America was at the root of all the world's problems. As a student of history, I often became engaged in intense arguments with him to prove that, in fact, the opposite was true.

Eventually I decided to write an entire book to prove my point. How elaborate a prank is that?

The Evil Empire: 101 Ways That England Ruined the World was published by Quirk Books and slated to be released on the queen's literal birthday, April 21, no less. It was brash. It said the British had invented slums and child labor, that they had burned Joan of Arc at the stake, put Saddam Hussein in power, and eventually colonized the entire globe just so they could drink tea.

I decided to take the troll even further. To promote the book, I produced an anonymous PSA and bought ad time on Fox News. It was made to look like a serious political advertisement, with people from all seven continents, Sunni, Hindi, Navajo, and others, claiming that they were putting aside their differences and uniting in one cause: to demand reparations from their longtime oppressor, the British Empire.

Thirty-one trillion pounds sterling, to be exact.

"A small sum for centuries of oppression and injustice," the commercial's voiceover intoned. "Britain has spent the last five hundred years ruining our world; it's time they pay the bill."

I timed it to run when Prince Charles was visiting Philadelphia that January. I also ran a full-page ad in the *Inquirer* that said he owed the entire planet those thirty-one trillion pounds sterling.

Apparently Prince Charles just happened to be watching TV when it ran. Of course, he also had the entire British press corps following him around. This immediately caused a shitstorm!

The next day, the *Daily Mail* ran a full-page story on the "controversy," written by the famous British historian Max Hastings. I was likewise slammed in the *Telegraph*. Then I got a call asking if I would drop everything and fly to the UK to be on *Richard & Judy*, a midday talk show kind of like the British version of *Oprah*. My stuffy fellow guests, all British, called it a "loo" book—as in, meant to be read only while taking a shit.

This was all great for me. An off-the-cuff troll among friends had gotten me the attention I craved.

Though it was still in preorders, the book shot to number one on Amazon and instantly became a hit in the UK too.

(Since then I've appeared on the BBC as an "esteemed American historian" twenty-two more times. It's hilarious.)

I started to realize that maybe I could start fucking with people in more focused ways.

Maybe I could even make it a part of my business plan.

PUMA AND CREATIVE GRENADES

THIS HAND-OVER-FIST MONEY we were making from R. J. Reynolds also allowed us to be a little ballsier with our other clients, namely, PUMA, which we had taken on in the mid-1990s.

"Dude, why are you bothering with PUMA?" a friend had asked me at the time. He worked for Wieden+Kennedy, Nike's agency. "PUMA is a loser brand."

I couldn't deny it. That was indeed how it was seen at the time.

But I knew that if I was successful with PUMA in facing off against the big dogs such as Nike and Adidas, then we would gain a creative reputation that would get us global brand work for years to come.

A lot of the tricks I now employ in the booze business I first discovered while with PUMA. They were almost like a startup back then. Their CEO was Jochen Zeitz, who was then just thirty years old (today he's the CEO of Harley-Davidson). Tony Bertone, their head of marketing, was a mere lad of only nineteen. At the time we started working with them, they were doing only around $30 million in annual sales, a pathetic number for a global fashion brand.

Fig. 11 The Dog Ate the Marketing Budget

(I'll interrupt myself to note that they had such a meager advertising budget, they offered to pay me in company stock, but I turned that down and insisted on cash. PUMA would later be sold to Gucci for $7.8 billion in 2007. Fuck me.)

When I look back on PUMA's strategy in the 1990s, the economic reality was that they couldn't afford to make any costly mistakes. So what they had to do was put out minuscule production runs of shoes and clothes, and if one sold out, then it sold out. But from an outsider's perspective, it looked as if they had a deliberate strategy to create scarcity.

From a marketing standpoint, we realized the best way to get people to talk about PUMA was to create constant news that would break through. We figured we could do that by making these limited runs for the coolest, most desirable stuff.

We started calling these releases *creative grenades.*

Sneakers are huge in fashion circles these days, of course, but back in the late 1990s, you simply didn't see them advertised this way. Ditto limited-edition "drops." So we got a ton of great press for every one of these creative grenades.

PUMA enlisted the minimalist German fashion designer Jil Sander to collaborate on a limited-edition women's running shoe. Essentially all she did was add a gold logo to a standard pair of running shoes, but people were obsessed.

We did one drop, timed during the 2002 World Cup, for "Shudoh" soccer cleats, which were available exclusively at high-end sushi restaurants in New York and

Japan. (That year's World Cup was held in Japan, you see.) We put the shoes in fancy bamboo-and-glass display cases and even had "Iron Chef" Morimoto make a limited-edition PUMA sushi roll to serve alongside them. Crazy stuff.

We bolstered that with a commercial that starred the British tough-guy actor (and former soccer player) Vinnie Jones (*Lock, Stock and Two Smoking Barrels*) and international soccer stars in an all-out Wild West shoot-out, except the whole fight took place in a chic sushi restaurant. For the PUMA-sponsored Cameroon team, we made a commercial using the kind of Japanese animation you typically saw only in video games at the time.

Another great example was a project we called PUMA Thrift. We made three hundred pairs of shoes using thrift-store clothing. We then turned these shoes into a traveling art installation exhibition. All the shoes sold out immediately.

No one else was doing such interesting stuff in the sneaker world during that era, so it became almost too easy to get buzz with these moves. We started seeing how insane we could be, how far we could push these creative grenades and still get coverage.

Fig. 12 FIFA Fair Play

For the launch of H-Street, a low-rise walking shoe, we literally sponsored the entire Jamaican Olympic team, and we had a real ball with it, garnering tons of press. A year after that, leading up to the 2004 Olympics in Athens, we did a series of TV spots where average citizens are surprised to be handed a relay-race baton by Jamaican athletes who would be competing in that summer's games. Little did we know it at the time, but one of them was a not-yet-famous Usain Bolt.

I think this Jamaica campaign was what single-handedly launched PUMA into the stratosphere globally.

After that, Tony had an idea for what he called the "96 Hours"—the thinking being, what if you needed a complete, custom-made wardrobe for, say, a four-day trip (do the math). You'd call in your measurements, and within four days we'd send you this beautiful titanium case, like James Bond or something, and inside it would be everything you'd need for a four-day/four-night trip. Four changes of clothes, business and casual, blazers and scarves, socks and underwear, and a couple pairs of shoes, of course. Even a toiletry bag and an alarm clock. Pretty cheeky.

It was insanely expensive, like $4,000, and we created every 96 Hours set on demand for each buyer.

We sold out immediately. Of course, no one actually needed this. Did anyone ever use the set for its stated purpose, or was it just a novelty purchase? I have no clue. But tons of journalists wrote about it.

And that is exactly the point of a creative grenade.

You get organic advertising without spending any of your own money (ad money that PUMA didn't even have at the time) and get people to start paying attention to your brand. Sure, we didn't expect average joes and janes to have any desire to buy or wear these shoes, or to buy a fuck-you expensive attaché case.

What we did expect was for them to read about these crazy items, however, and then go to their local Foot Locker to see the more normal, more affordable, but still very cool stuff PUMA was also doing at the time.

It must have worked, because starting in 2001, revenue at PUMA began tripling every single year.

Fig. 13 PUMA Gains Horsepower

We did one final ad campaign with PUMA in 2006, leading up to the World Cup in Germany. My favorite part of it was a crazy commercial for the Italian national soccer team, an almost Fellini-esque "day in the life" of these supercool athletes, shot by the great Swedish music video director Jonas Åkerlund. It must have been good luck because Forza Azzurri went on to win the World Cup.

By then, however, the stakes were getting too high—twelve different national teams wore PUMA jerseys at that World Cup!—and the brand was looking to sell. They weren't much interested in chance or fun or creative grenades any longer. Better to just play it safe and not risk doing something that would offend prospective corporate buyers.

That's what always happens, and why brands get less interesting as they find success and mainstream respect.

But it doesn't have to be that way.

You don't have to lose the stuff that makes a brand magical in the first place.

Fig. 14 Spare Key

PURSUING *BIKINI BANDITS,*
STARTING TO DO THINGS MY WAY

I STARTED MY AD AGENCY AT TWENTY-THREE.

I got married that same year.

I was reasonably wealthy by twenty-five.

And by thirty-two, I was having a midlife crisis.

My marriage had fallen apart, and I was still making a lot of money, but I was bored. Stuck doing the same old print ads and commercials. Even the occasional pranks weren't doing it for me anymore.

I thought, I just want to create some fun shit.

It was the summer of 1998, and my brother Pete and I were returning from a vacation in New Hampshire. Because of a thunderstorm, we were stuck on the airport runway for hours. We started drinking bourbon and ginger ales and goofing around. We decided there, on our seatback trays, to start writing a screenplay for a short film we'd surely never make.

We called it *Bikini Bandits,* and it was a rollicking caper about buxom thieves robbing convenience stores with semiautomatic weaponry while raising a whole lot of hell. It was an homage to the B-grade Russ Meyer movies and Van Halen videos we both loved. It was *Faster Pussycat! Kill! Kill!* meets "Hot for Teacher."

"You know, this is actually pretty good," I told Pete. (Maybe it was those bourbon and ginger ales talking.) "Why don't we just shoot this?"

It would be my greatest prank yet: an intentionally terrible movie meant to skewer Hollywood (and American consumer culture) while hopefully teaching me about the movie industry in the process.

I knew plenty of directors of photography because of all the commercials Gyro was making at the time. They could help me realize my vision. I also had an angle on some potential actors who could play the bandits.

You see, back then, we did the advertising for Delilah's Den, a local strip club in Philadelphia. They didn't pay us but instead offered us "trades." It's not what you think—it mostly meant my employees and I could come in whenever we wanted to drink beer and eat their crappy fried food.

We hired dancers from the club to star and ultimately shot something on the cheap and sent it to Atom Films, a cool indie film site that ran shorts produced by indie creators. They loved it! And so did their followers—it got something like thirty million views. That was big-time in the early days of the internet before YouTube.

Atom asked us to make more films and said this time they'd fund them. *Bikini Bandits and the Magic Lamp*. *Bikini Bandits and the Time Machine*. They flew us to Morocco to shoot a short, to Paris—you name it. We were only breaking even financially, but we were having a blast.

We started getting a reputation in the industry—these cool little filmmakers in Philadelphia, of all places. Hollywood A-listers started dropping by to visit us when they were in town. Maynard James Keenan from the band Tool. *Jackass*'s Johnny Knoxville. Jason Schwartzman of the band Phantom Planet and *Rushmore*. For a while, it was pretty fucking cool.

Then Atom said, "You should go to Hollywood and get some representation. That could lead to a feature film." Okay. So we flew out to Los Angeles, where every major talent agency wined and dined us. They sent flowers to my hotel room, lavished me with expensive bottles of cognac. We eventually went with United Talent Agency on the advice of a new friend, the great director Spike Jonze. For a while, Michael Ian Black and David Wain were attached to the script; they wanted to shoot the movie as a bit of a *Wet Hot American Summer*-type spoof.

Then . . .

. . . nothing happened.

Absolutely.

Nothing.

Fig. 15 The Movie Franchise That Never Was

You see, no one ever wants to say "yes" in Hollywood. There's just too much at stake. It's easier to give a soft "no" and just keep taking meetings.

Finally we found a savior in StudioCanal, the acclaimed French production company that had hit after hit in the 1990s. They wanted to make a *Bikini Bandits* movie in France with two of the hottest French celebrities of the moment: rapper JoeyStarr and Virginie Efira, who was then like the Paris Hilton of, uh, Paris.

They flew my new wife, Sonia, and me to France to meet the cast. They put us up in the hottest hotel in Paris, Hôtel Costes. When we went to eat with the cast and crew at the downstairs restaurant, literally every other diner would be staring at us. We were the coolest table at the coolest hotel in all of Paris.

After two epic dinners, *Bikini Bandits Save the World* was locked and loaded, ready to shoot.

I was set to direct it, and we were going to shoot in Réunion, an island off the coast of Madagascar that's part of the French Republic. Our plane tickets were already purchased. Everything was prepped.

Then it all fell apart.

Out of nowhere, the whole film just fucking collapsed.

The producer we were assigned to at StudioCanal had recently released a big-budget flop, and the studio was suddenly skittish with their money. We now had no one to fund the film and absolutely no budget.

We were fuuuuuuucked!

As the Hollywood dream disintegrated around me, I thought, How am I going to ever do this shit again?

I'd been trying to troll Hollywood, and instead I'd trolled myself.

I'd put so many hopes into this one stupid dream. And it had gotten me nowhere.

I had seen this great documentary about Orson Welles where he said the biggest regret of his life was putting so much effort into Hollywood.

Right then, I knew exactly what he meant.

Anything that requires so many people to have an opinion can never be any good.

From now on, I told myself, I'll always do things 100 percent my way.

And I was starting to realize there was one industry where I could actually pull that off.

REALIZING THAT ENCHANTMENT HAS DISAPPEARED, BRAND MYSTICISM IS THE KEY

As I was licking my wounds over *Bikini Bandits*, I started to really analyze why some things had worked so far in my young career . . . and why others hadn't.

In the beginning of my career, I was too intuitive. I didn't understand myself or my strategies. At the time, prospective brands would always say to me, "We love your work. How do we get that kind of work for ourselves?"

And . . . I never knew how to answer that.

Gyro Worldwide was never really about making money for me. I just didn't care. In retrospect, I now realize it was more like some giant conceptual performance art vehicle . . . that often just happened to make us really good money too.

But you can't say that in a business meeting.

So I'd just mumble something, and the would-be client would end up thinking we didn't actually know what the hell we were doing.

Eventually I started just admitting it: "I can't really tell you, I need to show you."

Obviously, that ambiguity doesn't work for everybody.

Then I read this great book called *As If* by Michael Saler. It really crystallized things for me. The basic gist of the book is that the Enlightenment and later the Industrial Revolution killed "magic" and "enchantment" in the world.

It turns out these two things are necessary for human existence.

We yearn for them.

We strive for them.

WE NEED THEM.

This became especially true after the Industrial Revolution. It was the dawn of a new age—God was dead!—and magic and mystery were being replaced with automation.

Suddenly people actually had time to kill.

Leisure time for the first time in human existence.

And, all of a sudden, things increasingly sucked because we had started destroying the sublime natural beauty around us.

What was left to enjoy?

What was there to do but sit in your office or, worse, stand at the assembly line in a factory?

It was not a coincidence that at the height of the Industrial Revolution, during the latter part of the nineteenth century, Jules Verne became a literary sensation. During this time, the Frenchman wrote nearly one hundred novels, many of which are still popular today, such as *Journey to the Center of the Earth*, *Twenty Thousand Leagues Under the Sea*, and *Around the World in 80 Days*.

These were fantastical stories that combined ideas of machinery, scientific discovery, and geographic exploration, complete with both real and made-up locations charted on highly detailed maps that were engraved throughout most of Verne's works.

Initially, Verne wrote these stories because he was so bored by his own life as a stockbroker in a stuffy Paris office. Writing about ballooning around the world, African safaris, and even space travel was his way to add enchantment to not just the doldrums of his own life but those of his (eventually) millions upon millions of worldwide readers.

And people loved it!

They were enchanted by these worlds. Sure, they were just described on a printed page, but they were like virtual reality for the mind.

Verne was called "the Man Who Invented the Future," "the Greatest of Dreamers," and eventually "the Father of Science Fiction." (Mind you, even after he became wildly successful, Verne rarely left France, and all these foreign places continued to come simply from his imagination.)

In his wake would arrive Sir Arthur Conan Doyle and his Sherlock Holmes saga, which had appeared by 1887; H. P. Lovecraft and his Cthulhu Mythos, which began in the pulp magazine *Weird Tales* in 1928; and, most significant to my future work, J. R. R. Tolkien's Middle Earth canon, which began in earnest with his 1937 children's book, *The Hobbit*.

All of these works, and even more modern ones such as *Star Wars*, *Harry Potter*, *Game of Thrones*, and, hell, even *The Simpsons*, enchant people because they offer layers of insane detail with maps; glossaries of weird, made-up languages and phrases; litanies of unique characters and dwellings—the whole nine yards.

They create their own mythologies.

It seems that the more details a creator adds to a story, the higher the level of engagement it will receive from readers, viewers, and fans. That's because it's seducing them with more overall enchantment.

The more enchantment, the stickier, the more pervasive the world becomes.

I started realizing that my greatest successes, my most viral brands, my most beloved creations were ones in which I had done just what Verne was doing, just what Tolkien was doing, just what Matt Groening and his team at *The Simpsons* were doing.

My great successes in advertising were because I had inadvertently created what I now call

Brand Mysticism.

My thinking is why can't a cigarette brand or a sneaker brand or, yes, a liquor brand be designed like a Jules Verne book, a George Lucas movie, a David Bowie album?

It's certainly counterintuitive to what they teach at Wharton.

But I didn't invent this idea. I just gave a name to it. It's always been true.

The most successful brands in the history of the world have an inherent weirdness and symbolism as part of their brand mystique. I think of Oreo's cookie design, which literally has baked (har!) into it the two-bar Cross of Lorraine, which was carried by the Knights Templar during the First Crusade, as well as the Cross Pattee, a symbol they wore on their white robes. Seriously, study an Oreo someday—there's a lot going on. It's not just a cookie.

Or look at Triscuit, seemingly a made-up word, but when it was created in 1903, it was a portmanteau of electricity and biscuit—these were the first crackers purported to be "baked by electricity."

As I was reading Saler's book, it was as if a lightbulb went off above my head. I thought, Aha! This is intuitively what we did with Red Kamel, what we did with PUMA, what I would eventually do with Hendrick's. In all these cases, sometimes accidentally, we created a world of enchantment that people could escape to, that they could become a part of. That they could essentially live in.

And that was what I should have been telling potential clients the entire time.

But it's not so easy to put into words. (I'm even having trouble right now.)

How did I tell clients that when they hired me and my company, they were signing up for a journey unlike any other they had ever been on, and for that reason, our process would be very different from that of any other ad agency they'd ever worked with?

Thinking about my work today, how do you tell a liquor company, which just wants to sell a few more bottles of vodka or whiskey, that we are going to create a fantastical new world for them? That, along with them, we are going to be the coauthors of wonderment? That it's going to take time and patience and trust in this strange process, a process that simply can't be measured by test groups or how many likes one brand post gets on Instagram?

It's so heady, so strange, so intimidating that it would surely make most clients go running out the door, eager to just throw money at a giant billboard or a pricey commercial during an NBA game.

The ones that don't run out the door, however, get enchantment.

Hendrick's did.

Sailor Jerry did.

So many others would.

It's been my guiding ethos ever since I realized it, and it's given me by far the greatest successes of my career. It's why you're even reading this book.

In Part II, for the first time ever, I'm going to give you a peek into how to enter that land of enchantment, that world of brand mysticism, via my work in booze.

Fig. 16 Bottleneck

II

MY BOOZE LIFE

I have woken up, emerged from the wilderness, or the underworld, and realized my mission in life. In this part of the book, I am now a wise old but still young man with a seemingly preternatural ability to create new gins, rums, whiskeys, and other alcoholic exotica and get everyone talking about them, buying them, drinking them, loving them. ☞Better put: this is all the crazy shit I did to—okay, I'll say it—revolutionize the modern world of alcohol brands.

STARTING MY BOOZE CAREER WITH A BANG

I ALWAYS SAY MY BOOZE career started with Hendrick's Gin, but that's not quite right.

Even when I was selling sneakers and smokes, I was also doing a little print work with Paddington Brands, which owned a lot of college-type shooters: Rumple Minze, Black Haus, and the like. For Goldschläger, a Swiss-produced cinnamon schnapps with literal gold flakes floating in it, I wrote a tagline I still love:

"Goldschläger, because Plutoniumschläger would kill you."

(No, I'm not the guy who said, "Let's put edible gold flakes in a liqueur." I'm just the guy who had to figure out how to sell it. Though I did learn that you can ingest 24K gold, but anything less pure is toxic. Oh, and for those of you who skipped Part I, welcome back.)

When our point man at Paddington left to work at William Grant & Sons, he gave us a little assignment for Glenfiddich. Then, as now, Glenfiddich was the biggest single malt scotch brand in the world. But both WGS and Glenfiddich were very, very sleepy at the time.

Single malt scotch already suffers from feeling geriatric and boring, but it was even worse two decades ago, when whiskey was not sexy whatsoever and was strictly for old men. I remember going to the Glenfiddich U.S. offices in Edison, New Jersey, and feeling like I'd somehow entered a portal and been taken back to 1964. Gross fluorescent lighting, drop ceilings, and a lot of Formica.

I really wanted to inject some personality into Glenfiddich, and I saw this as a great opportunity to make a splash in the booze world and potentially get more clients. So we designed a print campaign meant to sneak up on you. It ran in *Esquire*, the *Atlantic*, and lots of classy men's magazines.

If you didn't look closely, it appeared to be your standard-issue scotch ad. It showed a stuffy Scottish guy with his nose deep in a snifter of Glenfiddich Ancient Reserve 18 Year Old. The text noted that it took forever to create this special single malt matured in an Oloroso sherry cask, that Glenfiddich waited

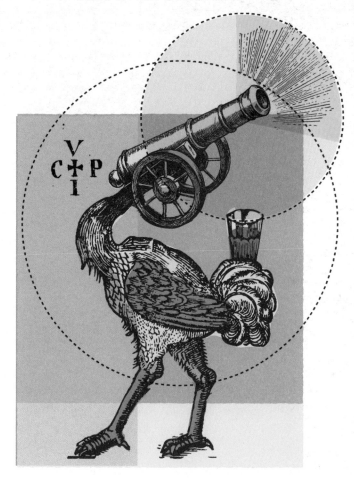

Fig. 17 Friendly Fire

for just the right time to release this beautiful scotch into the world. It explained how very crucial "patience and control" are in the single malt business.

Then the tag line, in big, bold letters:

"Tantric sex is a no-brainer for a whisky man."

I had just arrived on the booze scene...

THERE'S NOTHIN' BETTER THAN BOOZE

. . . AND NOW I WAS THERE TO STAY.

Because the fun I had with the Glenfiddich campaign and the buzz I received made me quickly realize something: The same effort and creativity I had put into something like *Bikini Bandits* could just as easily be put into selling booze, and more effectively too.

It's all just storytelling.

A booze brand done right has a deep, rich, sometimes epic story to tell you, just as a great film does.

Booze combines history and storytelling, two of my greatest passions.

People by and large love it.

Everyone has complaints after they watch a movie (too many plot holes, wooden acting, too long! It's always too long!).

Who bitches after having a great drink?

No one.

If I didn't already know it, Red Kamel made me realize that everyone hates you when you try to sell them cigarettes. And rightly so!

But everyone loves the spirits industry. It's an agricultural product, from the land, often uniquely local, and made by true craftsmen.

Of course, it makes people happy and fosters community.

And, unlike cigarettes, it has already gone through its Prohibition period, so all the regulations are already in place—you don't have to worry about the government coming down hard and crushing your industry one day just to make a few groups happy.

I probably don't have to tell you it has huge margins too. Movies are always in the red. But not booze!

And, unlike food, the product never goes bad. It can sit on the shelves for years, and it doesn't expire. Literally EVER. Imagine selling milk, knowing you have just a week to move it. Even with a book or a movie or a new clothing line, you basically have two months to recoup your investment before it is removed from shelves and taken off screens forever. Maybe you have only the single launch week these days. With streaming services, you might have only a launch day! Think how quickly something goes from the top listing on Netflix to impossible to even locate on the home page.

Whereas with booze, you have forever to sell it. You can test things, you can try things, you can keep plugging away until you finally nail it.

There's nothing else in the world quite like alcohol. There's never been a time in the history of the planet that people haven't loved booze. It literally never goes out of fashion . . . unlike fashion. When I did work for PUMA, man, if they didn't sell that shit in one season, it would end up in a landfill.

But booze is a combination of all the best qualities of all those other industries and art forms.

I feel that it is literally the best canvas in the world on which to project my creativity.

And through the years, I've learned you really need to have only four things in place to create a success in this arena.

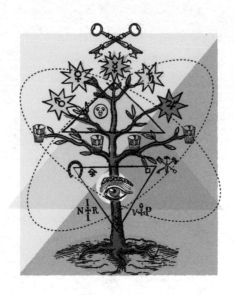

LESSON 1

THE FOUR MAGICAL INGREDIENTS IN A GREAT BOOZE BRAND

IF ALL THESE ARE IN PLACE, you might have a hit on your hands.

GOOD AND DIFFERENTIATED PRODUCT

GREAT PACKAGING

A COMPLEX BRAND WORLD

All three of these things need to work together to form one complete and cohesive idea.

The fourth ingredient is TIME

And the best part is that this formula, honed through my years in booze, will also work for whatever you're trying to sell, whether it be a totally different product or service, a broader creative message, or simply your own outward identity.

Throughout the rest of this book, we'll look at each of the four magical ingredients in closer detail.

HENDRICK'S—BEGINNER'S LUCK?

I DIDN'T EVEN KNOW how gin was made when Sir Charles Grant Gordon invited me to come to Scotland to see his "Gin Palace" in 1998.

William Grant & Sons was happy with my work with Glenfiddich, so they wanted to extend our relationship. Back then, WGS was run more like a mom-and-pop operation even though they were a major international spirits company, and Sir Charles was the head of the family firm.

"We need a gin," their execs told me.

At the time, they had plenty of whiskey but not a single gin in their portfolio. Okay.

"So do you have a flavor profile in mind?" I inquired.

No.

"An aesthetic?"

No.

"Do you even have a name?"

Nope.

It would be up to me and my fledgling company to create and consult on everything.

Perfect.

It was a daunting task, but I felt ready.

I flew into Dufftown, where the Glenfiddich Distillery is located, and was greeted by Sir Charles before we drove a camper van down to Girvan, an industrial town about sixty miles south of Glasgow. What I found there was hardly a palace; it was more like a garage with two old stills in it that Sir Charles had won in an auction after another distillery had shuttered back in 1966.

These stills, I'd later learn, were a 1948 John Dore Carter-Head and a Bennet copper pot still from the 1860s.

When I looked at these contraptions, with their balloon-shaped pots with odd cranks and gears, submarine-like hatches, and mazelike pipes with a lifetime of patina, I immediately thought of Jules Verne. The stills' aesthetic almost made me fantasize about climbing in and then traveling around the world or taking them deep under the sea.

I was enchanted by their beauty and even mystery, and I wanted that enchantment to translate to drinkers who, like me, would be unfamiliar with the magical world of gin production.

It wasn't all fantasy, though. The Carter-Head still had a gin basket, of course, where the botanicals are infused into the spirit.

"Can you put *anything* in there?" I asked. I really didn't know anything about gin. I was told, yes, you could. *Anything.* I would be sure to keep that in mind.

Eventually I returned to Philadelphia and started digging into history from the mid-1800s, when that Bennet gin still was designed and first used. I started by rereading Jules Verne, which led me to Victoriana, which took me to apothecaries of the era.

Inspired, I told my assistant at the time, Rona Harman—who is now president of our company—to go to some local antique stores and flea markets and buy any apothecary bottles she could find.

She came back at the end of the day with a few dozen. They had such interesting shapes. Some were bulbous, some like snow globes, others flat like a flask. They were made of brown glass and blue glass and other interesting colors you just don't see these days. I particularly liked one that was squat, rounded, tapered at the top, and made of forest-green, almost black glass, topped by a cork. There were no bottles on the market like that. So we went with it, and it's still the packaging you know today.

Ron Short—who has been with me since 1990 and even worked on the illustrations for this very book—was my original art director on Hendrick's. He and I were trying to evoke a "steampunk" vibe well before most people had ever heard the term.

The first (and only) focus group that we tested this packaging design on absolutely hated it, though.

The common reaction we got from them was "What the hell is this shit?" They were confounded and couldn't stop ripping on it.

Believe it or not, that made me know we were on to something big. If these people truly hated it so much, why were they still talking about it?

Flavor-wise, because I was still very naive about distilling, I suggested that they load the gin basket with freshly sliced cucumbers. Maybe that seemed very "gin-like" to me, or maybe I was thinking about my New Zealander wife, who loved the Pimm's cup, a British drink that is often served with freshly sliced cucumbers.

I also thought it had potential as the drink's bar call: "Give me a Hendrick's tonic with cucumber!" (From what I remember, Hendrick was the name of the Grants' longtime family gardener.)

Whatever the case, it was certainly a unique ingredient for a gin back then.

I suggested cucumbers to Lesley Gracie, master distiller at WGS, and, to my astonishment, she loved the idea. She, in turn, thought to use the essence of rose petals, evoking the very British idea of eating cucumber sandwiches in the flower garden. All credit due: She really made the recipe sing. No one had ever tasted a gin like this before, and that's why Lesley's recipe has since become globally renowned.

WGS seemed happy with our work and was willing to push the "go" button and take Hendrick's to market. They only gave us a tiny budget, however, so we had to create really cheap ads. We couldn't afford to use flashy photography or even any actors or sets. That was where the whole Terry Gilliam/*Monty Python's Flying Circus*-esque cutouts came from that we still use today. Every piece of art for the brand was handmade from old Victorian-era etchings.

All these strange little touches, all these disparate elements coming together—liquid, packaging, marketing, storytelling—really made Hendrick's stand out compared to the Beefeaters and Gordons of the world. Our wondrously weird gin was significantly more expensive as well.

Who would possibly buy it? It's not as if gin was red-hot at the time. It certainly had no luxury sector.

So what we did was we tried to turn Hendrick's oddballness into a positive.

My writer Jerry Stifelman, whom I have been continuously working with since 1991, came up with a great line for the ads:

"Loved by a tiny handful of people all over the world."

We turned the brand's polarizing nature into a challenge!

If you don't like Hendrick's, you're just not a part of our small, elite group. What is wrong with you?

Of course, it worked. (You wouldn't be reading this book if it hadn't.)

Now Hendrick's is on the back bar in every bar that matters in every corner of the world. It literally launched the craft gin craze, and today there are hundreds upon hundreds of boutique gin brands, all with weird flavor profiles, crazy bottles, and artsy packaging.

However, what makes Hendrick's continue to flourish over these copycats is the authentic brand world that WGS has allowed us to build over the last two decades. And it's why we've been able to transcend the "life cycle of hipness"—usually a few years—and withstand the onslaught of four hundred new gins being introduced every single year.

Even today, picking up a bottle of Hendrick's Gin manages to take you to that magical place I was taken when I first saw Sir Charles's stills nearly twenty-five years ago.

Fig. 18 The Original Globetrotter

A COMPLEX BRAND WORLD

Think Like Tolkien and Tool

AND THAT'S THE SECRET.

Brands need to be transportive.

My greatest successes happened after I realized that.

In fact, I feel like my booze brands are every bit as transportive as movies, music, and art.

A good brand can take you to another place, and if you enjoy staying there, you'll hopefully want to go back again and again.

Why was the Marlboro Man such a massive success? I hate to say it, but when you smoked a Marlboro, for those five minutes, you *were* the rugged Marlboro Man, roping cattle and riding bucking broncos, and all the women wanted to be with you.

After I read *As If*, I began to realize that this was what I had instinctively been doing with Red Kamel, and it was what I would also do with Hendrick's.

Think about it: Who else around the turn of the twenty-first century was creating mysticism around their gin brand? Around any of their booze brands, for that matter?

Certainly not the big boys. You might have enjoyed drinking Beefeater or Tanqueray, but what did it make you think of? Where did it transport you?

Nowhere.

While Hendrick's could make you feel as if you were in a nineteenth-century apothecary shop. Or as if you were riding some newfangled flying machine with Jules Verne. Or as if you were some retrofuturist steampunk going back in time to Victorian England.

People initially took a chance on the brand because they found it genuinely unique and interesting and tasty (especially compared to what was out there at the time), but they stuck with the brand as they learned that it became even more unique and interesting as they continued to explore it.

Upon discovering this, I knew it would be up to me and my team to make this brand infinitely, unyieldingly interesting for the rest of time. Our job with Hendrick's wasn't done merely because it was now on the market.

In fact, once Hendrick's first became a success on the drinks scene, I intentionally started doing more research on how novelists, filmmakers, and musicians created their insanely detailed worlds, seeing what I could cull from them.

In part because of my love for Led Zeppelin, who directly referenced J. R. R. Tolkien in several of their songs, I had been fascinated by the legendary fantasy author since childhood. He famously created his world's own language, Elvish, came up with an alphabet, and even built a "Tree of Tongues" to chart his constructed language from the source. He drew maps for imaginary lands and sketched landscapes, dwellings, and environments. He came up with characters, all with rich backstories, cultures, and beliefs, ones that, in many cases, only Tolkien himself would ever even know about.

Tolkien began creating, imagining, and consuming himself with this immense world twenty-five years before he ever put pen to paper to write *The Lord of the Rings*—which would take him another twelve years to finish. Imagine!

And that's why it remains so vital today.

Star Trek and *Star Wars* work the same way. Think of how many characters, landscapes, vessels, planets, and worlds you can recall from those two series. Even if you're not some Trekker or *Star Wars* nerd, they're so rich that you can't help but have had them infect your consciousness. That's why they feel so real to the obsessives, many of whom truly think they are Jedis or whatever.

As I hinted in Part I, in many cases, these fantasy worlds emerged during bleak times in human history. Jules Verne's came after industrialization had created a desire and need for leisure time, a wish to escape to fantastical worlds different from our own. Tolkien's came after the Great Depression and in between two World Wars. *Star Trek* hit the airwaves as U.S. troop involvement was ramping up in Vietnam while Civil Rights protests were intensifying back home.

The present day has given us tragedy after tragedy, struggle after struggle, chronically reported by the twenty-four-hour news cycle and social media.

People want to escape now more than ever!

What we've done with the Hendrick's brand world is create something that transcends the liquid; that's something you can do only if you're ignoring the market, if you're not chasing trends, which to me is the worst thing you can ever do when starting a brand.

That's also why, when WGS started creating and releasing new variants of Hendrick's in 2019, we felt it was important that they weren't just saying to Lesley, "Oh, now we need you to do a barrel-aged version of Hendrick's." Or "We need to do a 'Japanese' Hendrick's gin since Japanese spirits are so hot—just add yuzu!"

No!

That's what everybody else would do.

The Hendrick's product extensions had to be based on extending the boundaries of the crazy brand world itself. For the first one, Hendrick's Orbium, for example, Lesley produced what she called a "quininated" gin—one made with additional extracts of quinine—and so we explored what Hendrick's might taste like in a parallel universe. How cool is that?

(And if it becomes a hit, how would other brands even rip us off?)

Hendrick's Midsummer Solstice was meant to be enjoyed during a flowery summertime event like a wedding. Hendrick's Amazonia Gin was designed by Lesley to evoke the botanicals of the Amazon jungle. Hendrick's Lunar Gin, released in early 2021, was a spirit meant to be drunk while "moon-bathing," as we called it, at night.

Ideas like those are why I believe Hendrick's—or Verne or Tolkien or *Star Wars*—will never go out of style. Because they—*we*—are not trying to beat the young whippersnappers at the game. They're writing their own rule book.

Ever see an aging band trying to fit in with the current market and appeal to youth? They look like idiots!

A band (and a brand) needs to know itself and its fans.

One of my favorite examples of this idea of brand mysticism is the band Tool. Their 2019 album *Fear Inoculum* came out thirteen years after their previous album, and it was one of their best, I felt. But *Pitchfork* destroyed the album, giving it 5.4 out of 10, with the critic saying it wasn't on trend; it could have come out any time over the last twenty years, and it wouldn't have mattered.

That's the point, dummy!

Tool is not trying to inhabit bullshit music trends.

Tool remains magical because stylistically they are 1970s prog rock mashed up with modern heavy metal. You can't pin them down. Each album is Byzantine in structure and hard to decipher—I heard one critic call their albums "Rubik's cubes." In other words, something to struggle to figure out, to take years to master, if you ever do.

Angry metalheads love Tool, but so do art world intellectuals due to the beauty and mystique of their music (not to mention their insane stop-motion music videos from back in the day). They aren't above trolling their audience either, once claiming to be practitioners of something called "lachrymology," supposedly the science of crying—people eventually figured out that that was bullshit.

(I should mention that I came to be friends with Maynard James Keenan after we crossed paths in the *Bikini Bandits* days, and in many ways, I consider him a mentor when it comes to this branding theory.)

You see, Tool knows who they are. They know what distinctive world they have created. You might even say that Tool is a genre unto themselves.

And you don't have to like them!

But their true fans love them. Despite lukewarm reviews from critics such as that *Pitchfork* guy, fans packed arenas for the *Fear Inoculum* tour, which knocked Taylor Swift out of the number-one spot on the album charts and ended up being the third-best-selling album of the entire year. And when Tool finally offered their back catalog on streaming services that same year, 1996's *Ænima* reentered the Billboard top 10 albums chart, and 1993's *Undertow*, 2001's *Lateralus*, and 2006's *10,000 Days* landed in the top 20. The albums truly were timeless.

I'm inspired by Tool's thinking, artistry, and longevity and want the same for my brands.

Just like Tool, Hendrick's doesn't chase the market and doesn't care what the mainstream thinks.

All we care about is transporting you out of the present.

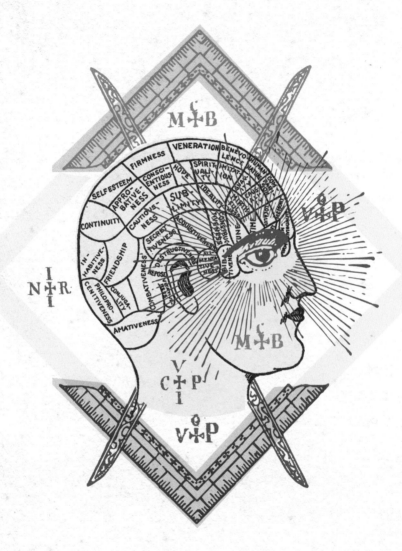

Fig. 19 Mapping the Mind

A GREAT BRAND WORLD EXTENDS TO YOUR CREATIVE TEAM TOO

I'M NOT A MASSIVE FAN of Springsteen's music, but his documentary *Letter to You* really spoke to me. Bruce knows who he is and how he's perceived, and that is why he's able to keep his brand alive and strong.

He has held the E Street Band together for fifty years. They've become fine-tuned instruments that know each other inside and out. Even when Clarence Clemons died, his nephew Jake took over his place in the band—and I don't think that was for the optics either. They wanted to keep the family together.

I first learned about that in the documentary and thought, My god! That's what I have been able to do with my team too. We have eighty-five employees; twenty of them have been with me for over fifteen years, and five of them have been with me for over twenty-five.

By keeping the team together, we're simultaneously able to maintain and keep alive the culture and mission of Hendrick's and our other clients.

That's what you have to do in order to succeed.

That's because this mysticism, these brand worlds we create, is so elaborate that a lot of the time they exist only in my head and the heads of my core team. We have this mind-meld thing going on where we always seem to know where we're headed and what comes next.

And that's why I can be so loud and sure of myself in a meeting when someone pitches a new idea or strategy for Hendrick's.

"That won't work!" I'll interrupt.

"Why?"

"Because that's not what Hendrick's *is*."

But they might not get it.

Of course, the more you are able to clearly articulate what your brand is, the more leeway your clients will give you to keep doing what you're doing.

I think of David Simon, the mastermind behind *The Wire*, who prepared an eighty-page "bible" for his pitch to HBO. By then, he had already envisioned dozens of characters, settings, episodes, and even full seasons into the future. I have to think he wouldn't have been able to convince them to take on such an atypical, heady, *dense* show otherwise.

We too will at times put down a bible for how we see a brand that is a mixture of words, images, music, and impressions. It's very artistic, and it always requires a certain kind of 4D thinking.

Of course, all this can work only if you have fully harnessed your ideas about the brand and you are likewise able to have full creative control over it. Which, you won't be surprised to hear, is often a rarity in the world of big multinational conglomerates that make decisions by committee with oversight from a team of C-suite execs, company lawyers, and shareholders. The fact that WGS is family-owned, with an amazing team and culture, is a big reason that Hendrick's continues to be what it is. So over the last two decades, WGS has allowed us to write their story and maintain that consistency.

What other booze brands have possibly had the same auteur, the same creative group, for so long? Not many that I can think of. (This goes along with my Onion Method, which I'll discuss in a bit.)

Hendrick's corporate brand team in Ireland gets all these agencies calling from all over the world, trying to steal the account from us. But, as far as I know, they've never considered dropping Quaker City Mercantile, which is what Gyro Worldwide eventually became (a story I'll get into later). That's just a special relationship that we've earned.

Twenty-two straight years of double-digit growth, year after year, helps too.

And, after all this time, there is no one on this planet that understands the brand world as well as I and my team do . . . because we created it.

That's what ultimately was the death knell for Red Kamel. I had built a brand mysticism with all these intricate stories, all this meticulous level of detail; a brand personality with its own backstory. And it worked!

But a big, publicly listed company such as R. J. Reynolds can't seem to help themselves. I'm not sure why they do this, but they seem to have this insatiable need to bring in a new regime every few years and blow up everything that was done before. Thus, shortly after R. J. Reynolds combined with British American Tobacco in 2004, they killed off Red Kamel.

Generally, though, creating these intensely detailed worlds is good for your business. Because it makes you indispensable. As long as that brand survives, it needs you there to feed it. And the more elaborate the brand world you've created, the harder it will be for another agency to steal it from you. That goes for anything creative—TV show, film, tech startup, whatever.

The more you are the author of something, the harder it is for someone else to take it over. You've created these magical detailed maps of Middle Earth—whatever "Middle Earth" may mean for your project—and no other person, no other agency can just march in and say, "No! Middle Earth should actually look like *this*."

Well, how do you know?

You didn't build it.

I did.

SAILOR JERRY RUM

A Punk Rock Captain Morgan at the Perfect Time

THE SAME EXACT DAY that they told me they needed that gin, William Grant & Sons also told me they needed a rum brand.

Same deal.

This time, though, I immediately had an idea.

Among the tattoo crowd, Norman Keith Collins was the Godfather. He had been a tattoo artist in postwar Hawaii, known for expanding the color palette of the tattoos he gave as he defined a nautical-inspired, visual vocabulary of sparrows, flying skulls, clipper ships, pinup girls, and, yes, bottles of booze. They called him "Sailor Jerry," but he was hardly a household name when he died of a heart attack in 1973, though he was a legend on the World War II/merchant marine/tattoo scene.

That scene was still pretty tiny and hardly mainstream. Even around 1997, when one of my acquaintances at the time, a burly tattooed fella, introduced me to the world of Sailor Jerry and suggested that we start a clothing line based on it, tattoo culture in America was hardly as ubiquitous as it is today.

But I liked its potential.

By then, one of Sailor Jerry's protégés that you've probably heard of, Ed Hardy, and another you might not have, Mike "Rollo" Malone, had taken over Collins's tattoo parlor and control of his estate, which included letters, artwork, and tattoo flash. Not much was happening with it, though.

It felt like undiscovered American folk art to me. I thought it deserved to be celebrated.

In 1997, I bought the Sailor Jerry trademark from Ed and Rollo for an, as they say, "undisclosed amount." I started a clothing line using Norman Collins's aesthetic and even his artwork, which I now owned. (This was before Hardy launched his own clothing brand.) This brand was doing alright, but it was hardly a worldwide sensation. We'd gone so far as to set up a retail location in Center City, right below our new Gyro Worldwide offices, and were hoping to attract more customers.

So when WGS asked for a rum idea, I had one that would solve two problems.

"Let's make a rum and call it Sailor Jerry," I told WGS. "And maybe it will help us sell some of these clothes," I whispered to my business partners.

Yes, we literally licensed our own trademark to William Grant & Sons.

(And as a result, I'd end up getting royalties on each and every bottle sold.)

That's a lot of chutzpah. They tell you to create a rum, and you name it after something you already own.

But it worked!

The company branding and aesthetic would now be based on something unique, historical, and authentic, but . . .

We still needed a unique liquid profile, of course.

My first thought was: How the hell do we beat Captain Morgan?

They were and are, by far, the biggest spiced rum brand in the category.

The answer, of course, is that we didn't. You can't beat Captain Morgan. Average joes already love it. It's all they even know. "Gimme a Captain and Coke" is one of the most ubiquitous drink calls in America.

But Captain Morgan is only 70 proof. What kind of hard-partying rum drinker wants such a measly proof?

What if we made our Sailor Jerry Rum higher-proof?

So we took it up to 92 proof and started positioning it as a higher-octane Captain Morgan (and for just a buck more a bottle). Instead of fucking pirates, we had hula girls and old-school tattoo culture.

It was a simple idea.

A punk rock Captain Morgan.

But we also got lucky—the international beverage conglomerate Diageo had just formed in 1997 and by 2000 had acquired Seagram's, which had Captain Morgan in their portfolio. Suddenly a lot of distributors that had relied on Captain Morgan lost it and now needed a spiced rum replacement.

We fit the bill.

I certainly understand how critical luck can be in determining your fortune. In fact, I think the ability to capitalize on luck is an important lesson. It's like being a surfer waiting for the perfect wave. The timing of the wave is luck, but when it comes, you'd better be ready, in the necessary position to catch it, and capable of surfing it.

Luckily, we were.

In this case, the wave started building with our new distributor in the Midwest. They were likewise pissed that Captain Morgan and Diageo had abandoned them, so much so that they would do anything they could to kick that drunk pirate's ass. So they pushed Sailor Jerry like crazy throughout middle America, especially in college towns such as Madison, Wisconsin, where it became a sensation.

We never beat Captain Morgan, but today Sailor Jerry is number two in the category and a household name. Not half bad.

★ THE MAGICAL INGREDIENT ★

GREAT PACKAGING

Make It Ugly on Purpose

I THINK ONE BIG REASON Sailor Jerry succeeded is that we intentionally made its packaging kind of shitty. It looks like it's straight off the shelf of your grandpop's basement bar.

For the logo, we used one of Norman Collins's more cliché tattoos and certainly one of my least favorite—a busty hula girl. It wasn't even the right shape for the label. The words barely fit beside it.

If you really think about it, it doesn't make sense either! The rum is distilled in the Caribbean (and bottled in Scotland), so why is a Hawaiian hula girl on there?

It's always made me think of my favorite Malcolm McLaren quotation: "The popularity of punk rock was, in effect, due to the fact that it made ugliness beautiful."

(McLaren, of course, was the genius impresario behind the Sex Pistols and Bow Wow Wow. There's that punk rock attitude again.)

As I keep saying, I don't care if something is trendy because I don't want our brands to be trendy. In fact, being right on trend is a sign of failure for me. Great

Fig. 20 My Favorite Cryptid

packaging should transcend the ages, not be of the moment. I want my brands not only to last one hundred years but to look as if they have already been around for one hundred years. I don't want to win a gold pencil or whatever the fuck it is they give away at the British Design and Art Direction Awards or the One Show.

I've given many interviews railing on British design firms before. To me, much of their design work just feels so "design-y" and trendy, which means it will probably look dated and godawful in a year. A few years, if they are lucky.

In fairness, American agencies tend to be kinda like 'Murica itself—simple and stoopid. But British firms are way too stylish for their own good.

(Yes, okay, I have a bee in my bonnet about the British. Again, see *The Evil Empire*.)

My view on visual creation is deeply personal. I create only things that I generally find interesting. That's my biggest rule: Create what's interesting to you. Not your boss or award show juries but you!

Unfortunately, most people don't actually know, much less have the courage to figure out, what they find interesting.

Luckily, I do know what interests me: history.

As a history nerd, I didn't see Sailor Jerry as just some unknown tattoo guy; I saw him more as an American folk artist through the lens of the Smithsonian and World War II. That was my jumping-off point. Because of that, even though his name was now on millions of bottles of Caribbean rum sold by a massive Scottish company, it would still feel underground and have a deep sense of authenticity.

Treating it like folk art is what has kept the Sailor Jerry brand from having the same fate as Ed Hardy's clothing line, which seemed too of the moment and quickly fell into the dustbin of fashion.

But my experience with Red Kamel taught me that simply reviving an old label or an old logo wasn't a guarantee of longevity or success. You realize pretty quickly that old stuff, when unaltered, can look a little too frumpy.

But when you mash up something old with something else, maybe even something new, it immediately has a cool vibe. It's almost a trick of the mind.

"Where did that come from?" people will wonder.

Suddenly there's not just a historical mystique but something that feels modern and as if it has an inherent truth to it. You need to have some degree of truth in order for your brand to resonate with people. Everything branches out from that inherent truth.

So that's the key trick we've employed over the years when it comes to our design work: We make it ugly on purpose.

By ugly I don't necessarily mean unattractive. By ugly I mean decidedly not trendy, not "cool," not of the moment, not fucking zeitgeist-y. Instead, we try to make it look authentic to an era or genre or idea that we are trying to evoke. That reads as ugly to most people in advertising, but it's beautiful to me.

That's exactly what we did with Sailor Jerry. Exactly what we did with Hendrick's Gin. Exactly what we now do with all of the brands we work on.

We purposely do not look at any design trends.

We want our brands to evoke an ambiguous period that they're inspired by, during which they're supposed to have been created.

I've had people flat-out tell me, "You couldn't have possibly created Hendrick's—it's from the 1800s!"

I love that!

You know you've done a good job with your branding when people literally can't tell what era it spawned from.

They see the old-timey apothecary bottle from the 1830s, the penny-farthing iconography from the 1870s, the Monty Python cartooning from the 1960s, all wrapped around a gin created in the late 1990s and now advertised in 2022. It fucks with the mind!

And that's great for branding.

ADVERTISING AWARDS ARE WORTHLESS

Sailor Jerry is never going to win a design award.

(Not that we'd ever enter it in a contest.)

But that's a good thing.

If you want to create original, unique things, your mind needs to be devoid of the influence and noise of your peers.

The advertising industry, for one, is full of people talking among themselves about themselves.

And all they're trying to do is mimic one another.

Trying to mimic each other while being just a *haaaaaaaaaaaaaaaaaaair* better.

That's why advertising award shows are such a fucking waste of time and money. It's ad people entering their own ads (with a hefty entry fee) to be judged by other ad people who think exactly like they do. It's a circle jerk.

Why would I want to impress ad people? Let's face it, most of these people were nerds in high school, and nobody liked them. That's why their "funny" ads are never really all that funny and their "clever" ads are never really all that clever and their "cool" ads are just plain dorky. I mean, how cool can an ad for toothpaste be?

The truth is, I don't spend much time thinking about ads. From my experience, advertising alone doesn't do that much to move the needle in terms of sales for a product. Think about some of the funniest commercials you can recall. You probably can't remember what brand they were for.

What matters instead is creating a cohesive and immersive brand world where every single element from the matchbook cover to the T-shirt to the package design to the in-store display to, yes, even the advertising is all working together and is connected.

All the pieces need to add up.

Would the work we have done for Hendrick's over the past two decades have won some awards if we'd entered it into these dog-and-pony shows? Maybe. Probably. But who the fuck cares? I know I sure don't. It's all just a distraction.

I think these beliefs started forming in me when I was working with R. J. Reynolds. We were such pariahs in the ad world that I couldn't have entered the stupid award shows even if I had wanted to.

Right from the get-go at Quaker City Mercantile, I told my team we weren't going to bother with any of the award shit. I told them it takes bigger balls to make things that are so off-trend that people at other ad agencies won't even understand them. Wouldn't possibly want to give them awards. Might even think they suck!

There's a trick to winning awards: You need to make your creative work a certain way in order for the judges to award it. You're speaking to that panel, not to your actual audience. And that goes against what we intend to do.

I'm admittedly not a designer, but I work very closely with my designers. I think I also have a knack for what looks and feels authentic. Recently we hired a new art director. In the interview, he told me he wanted to work with us because, and I quote, "Your stuff has a certain scuzz to it."

Why, thank you!

Award shows don't give prizes to scuzz, though.

Award shows give prizes to those who most closely mimic what's fashionable at any given time.

To make something ugly on purpose takes real balls. To put something into the world like the original Sailor Jerry packaging, which looked like an old man's design from the 1950s? That felt courageous. We knew it wouldn't win any design awards.

But I knew we'd have the last laugh. And I think we have.

Fig. 21 Another One for the Trophy Case

Fig. 22 No More Tears

MY ONION METHOD

Speaking of design awards, many marketing people focus almost completely on what we call "above the line" work. TV commercials, glossy spreads in magazines, billboards in Times Square and on the Sunset Strip. You know, the sexy stuff!

But I know that chances are the first time someone encounters one of my brands, it will more likely be "below the line"—in other words, at a physical establishment. It won't necessarily be on the back bar at a trendy cocktail lounge, but maybe they'll see our logoed coaster or matchbooks when their beer is set down at their local pub, or they'll notice our display at a neighborhood liquor store or airport duty-free shop.

Now, most brands have different marketing agencies that handle that sexy above-the-line work and the more meat-and-potatoes below-the-line work. Not at Quaker City Mercantile. We insist on doing *everything*.

That's because I truly believe that the small details of a brand are just as important as the big, flashy stuff. The small details are what ultimately make a brand stick. So QCM insists on doing the packaging, the swag, the store displays, the print ads, the TV commercials, the social media posts . . . and, yes, even the coasters and matchbooks.

This is what I call my Onion Method.

If enchantment is my idea that great brands can be transportive in the same way as a Jules Verne book or *Star Wars* film, then the Onion Method is how I achieve that: by building layer upon layer of meaning and weirdness into a brand's mysticism.

There is a ton of symbolism surrounding the humble onion, even in its name. The word "onion" is derived from the Latin word *unio*, meaning "union" or "unity." The onion has long been considered a mystical object; who doesn't know the metaphor of peeling an onion to find hidden layers, uncovered truths?

The ancient Egyptians worshiped onions, taking sacred oaths with their right hand on an onion in the belief that the perpetual circle-within-a-circle design symbolized eternal life. Pharaohs were even buried with onions over their eyes, against their ears, and over their pelvic regions.

It wasn't just the Egyptians. The ancient Greeks practiced cromniomancy, translated as "onion oracle"—in other words, divination by onions. This practice would eventually spread across Europe, Africa, and Asia and is something you can still see today in the form of Russian Orthodox churches' iconic onion domes.

I find this shit so profound.

But for my work, the Onion Method simply means ensuring that every single part of a brand works together in concert. With great brands, the more you scratch the surface, the more layers you peel off, the more there is to find inside, and the more interesting it gets.

The *weirder* it gets.

Here's a great example: Early on with Hendrick's Gin, WGS released a little book called *Field Guide to Hendrick's*. It was incredibly elaborate, insanely complex, so fucking expensive to produce that we printed only a few of them. Hardcover, hand-sewn binding, and nearly one hundred pages of content about this fairly new gin brand.

There were beautiful drawings on every page, discussions of obscure botanicals, cheeky ideas for party games ("bobbing for cucumbers" was one), discussions of crazy inventions such as the Pianocktail ("whose ivory keys have been carefully calibrated to mix a different cocktail in accordance to the tune that is played"), and cocktail recipes from top bartenders such as Dale DeGroff.

Spirits and cocktail books may be common these days, but you have to remember, back in 2005 when we released the *Field Guide*, they simply didn't exist. (David Wondrich's seminal *Imbibe!*, which really kicked off the modern cocktail book trend, wouldn't come until 2007.) So it made absolutely no sense to create something like this that really only a few people on planet Earth would possibly want.

But the thing was: THEY WERE THE RIGHT PEOPLE.

Fig. 23 Ouroboros for Two

We had banked on that. The first chapter of the *Field Guide* was even called "Hendrick's—It's Not for Everyone." So it became a huge sensation in the hippest parts of London, a huge part of the brand's early underground buzz in the UK. We even got a request from Harvey Nichols, a posh department store chain, to sell the *Field Guide* in their stores.

You see, fans thirst for more information about the things they are truly obsessed with. And our biggest fans wanted to peel back the layers of the Hendrick's onion until they reached the tiniest core. To people like them, a compelling booze brand like Hendrick's was akin to a great book that you could also drink.

So many brands out there are just surface. Even very successful ones. It's this hipster Brooklyn aesthetic I detest that is so of the moment, so zeitgeist-y, so fucking Goopable. Mattresses in a box, hemp shoes you order off Instagram, viral suitcases made from recycled water bottles.

I call these companies blands. Not brands.

Sure, all this stuff looks cool; it has all the right lettering and packaging and belief system ("We source the finest...blah blah blah...handcrafting it from blah blah blah"), but you dig deeper and there's really nothing there. It's bland. They could easily have been created by some sort of trend robot. And within a couple of years, no one will even remember them anymore.

They're Potemkin brands. Merely a facade. They couldn't produce a one-hundred-page field guide about themselves because they have nothing to say.

They may be trendy for the moment, but they have no layers. No soul.

They have no mysticism.

They aren't an onion.

Moral of the story: There is always going to be someone out there who is trendier than you. There are always going to be brands out there that have more Wharton MBAs working for them. But I feel confident that no one can outweird Hendrick's because we are coming from a totally unique place that transcends style.

Thus, long after that sleek CBD soda ("handcrafted in DUMBO, Brooklyn") has spun through its life cycle of hipness, Hendrick's will still be around.

Another story: When WGS bought out our shares of Sailor Jerry in 2008, they spent a great deal of time and effort trying to figure out what was making the brand so sticky in certain parts of the country and among certain groups of people. They wanted to home in on the ONE KEY REASON it was going viral in those particular circles.

And I kept telling them: There isn't one key reason.

It was everything we'd been doing, big and small.

If you discovered Sailor Jerry at a party and had no idea who Norman Collins was but then went on our website, you would think, "Holy shit! This brand is cool."

If you were an old school tattoo fan and went on our website wondering why a rum brand was named after a salty tattoo artist, you would then learn about all these cool bands that were drinking our stuff.

But WGS didn't quite believe me and ended up spending quite a bit of money without learning much.

I firmly believe that the deeper you dig into a brand, the more interesting it has to become. It's the same way in the art world.

Think about Tolkien.

Think about David Bowie.

If you say the world has changed from their day, I disagree. In the present, look at one of my filmmaking idols, Christopher Nolan. He, of course, doesn't use the term Onion Method, but he clearly believes in it and lets it inform his work. I saw an interview where he explained that people these days tend to watch movies more than once, thanks to the readily available streaming platforms and all the chopped-up clips and GIFs and memes that pervade the internet. That's why he believes it's his responsibility to make films that have multiple layers in their narrative, that have ambiguity and mystery and mysticism.

"If you watch it a second time, you're going to watch them in a slightly different way," Nolan claimed.

Think about that the next time you come across *Inception* or *Interstellar*. You're captivated. You might not even be sure you like it. But next thing you know, you're on Reddit or some random blog, reading what others are saying about it, learning about theories and Easter eggs, and contributing your own thoughts to the discourse.

Someone makes a crazy point. ("Kat is actually Neil's mother in the past!") Now you immediately want—no, need!—to rewatch *Tenet* so you can reassess things. Soon you're discovering more about the movie, not less. (How many movies are great the first time, and then you rewatch them and see that you were simply duped by meaningless spectacle or a tacked-on twist ending?)

Nolan's movies stay with you, become a part of you, because he follows the Onion Method.

But this can be very hard to drive home to the companies we work with.

"What's the point of going to all the expense and trouble?" they ask. They'd rather spend the money on market research.

They'd love for us to just shut up and create a vodka label or whatever and then hand it over to their marketing team. But you can't create an onion that way.

These companies just don't get why we need to add such complexity to a simple bourbon release or a new canned cocktail.

"Does anyone really care?" they'll say.

And the fact is, NO, many people don't care. Our clients are sorta right.

Likewise, would *Inception* have been a cool movie if it was just Leonardo DiCaprio running through people's dreams? Sure.

Would Bowie have been a rock star if his aesthetic and ethos weren't a mash-up of his incredible knowledge of the strangest parts of the world? You bet.

Would *The Lord of the Rings* still have been an entertaining story without all of Tolkien's maps and Elvish and world building?

Probably.

But I don't think *Inception* posters would be hanging in dorm rooms and Bowie would have a worldwide museum retrospective after his death if they hadn't followed the Onion Method. I don't think *The Lord of the Rings* would be a masterpiece that still lives on today, that is still adapted for new media half a century after Tolkien's death, that still inspires fanfic and resonates profoundly with new fans who discover it every single year, if Tolkien hadn't built it like an onion.

Sure, most people who liked Hendrick's at the start had no need for an esoteric *Field Guide*.

But the people who did care cared so much that they became Hendrick's evangelists on the London scene. They were the ones who ultimately made the brand a worldwide success and I'm sure are still sticking with it two decades later.

They are still trying to peel away even more layers of the onion to see what else is hidden inside, waiting to be revealed.

Fig. 24 Fun and Games

ENJOY GYROMART.COM

DEEZ NUTS AND THE VALUE OF PERFORMANCE ART

EVERYTHING YOU CREATE IN LIFE, however, doesn't need to begin as part of some grand master plan.

You don't always need to be building an onion, and I'm not contradicting myself when I say that.

It's okay to make stuff that might not ever even make you any money. The pranks and trolls I mentioned in Part I, for instance. In its later days, Gyro Worldwide would become famous for what I now realize was some pretty great performance art.

You might wonder how performance art would have any place in the world of a profitable business. In the world of cost-cutting, VC-funded companies, it doesn't. In my life, though, I now find it critical for figuring out how the world actually works.

That was the thinking behind G*Mart, Gyro Worldwide's pop-up convenience store that we opened in 1999. If our *Bikini Bandits* shorts were partially a commentary on the grotesqueries of American consumer culture, the G*Mart store that the buxom bandits were always shooting up was a spoof on the ubiquitous Walmart we all loathed. G*Mart became such a "character" in the films that we wanted to see what it would feel like to walk into one in real life.

How would the culture react if we tossed an entire store-sized creative grenade into the heart of Philadelphia?

We, yet again, took some of the ample fees we were making from Big Tobacco and opened up G*Mart on 38 North Third Street in Old City.

As far as I know, G*Mart was the first guerrilla pop-up store/art installation anywhere in the world, seven or eight years before that hipster Dave Eggers started opening superhero and pirate supply stores in New York and San Francisco.

You see these "fake" businesses all the time today. They're so cheesy, so meant to be Instagrammed. Maybe a coffee shop will become the *Friends* coffee shop to promote a new streaming release or whatever, and all the lame tourists will line up. But this was a pop-up shop for a movie no one had ever seen.

And if you came into the G*Mart, you wouldn't find Mountain Dew or Slim Jims. Instead, you'd find fake products such as Deez Nuts and Holy Water. Or crass T-shirts we designed.

We ran crazy, almost hypnotic ads on local radio stations that kept repeating nonsensical phrases ("*master baker . . . master baker . . . master baker*") and were full of masturbatory double entendres even worse than that. In the back of the store, we even had a performance space. On the first Friday of every month, bands would play G*Mart. People on the street would come in looking for some Doritos and be totally confused to find a full-on hip-hop concert noisily going on in the back room.

One time we even had Jason Schwartzman's band, Phantom Planet, which famously did the theme song for the TV show *The O.C.* The band eventually did an entire G*Mart-themed music video for their song "Hey Now Girl." And

Maynard James Keenan wore our G*Mart ringer tee on the cover of *Spin* magazine in 2001.

G*Mart eventually became the epicenter for the coolest people in town.

I even met my second and current wife, Sonia, there.

It was a blast, but we also began using it as a bit of a workshop to tinker with and learn how the retail business actually worked. At first, the only "real" products we sold were R. J. Reynolds cigarettes. Walls of them. It was like a cigarette showroom. By then, it was getting hard to find unique (and legal) ways to advertise cigarettes, so why not find a unique way to sell them instead—literally controlling the point of sale?

It was a very successful strategy, and I wondered if we could do the same for PUMA. I somehow talked the company into letting me be the exclusive retailer for their most limited drops. Because of our relationship with them, because we had access to their international catalog, we were soon stocking PUMAs that no other store in the United States had.

This was right before the internet changed sneakerhead culture, so people would travel to G*Mart from New York in the north and Washington in the south just to buy hot sneakers.

Soon enough, our performance art project had turned into the top PUMA retailer in the entire country, and G*Mart was making around $60,000 in monthly sales. We did so well with PUMA, in fact, that it became detrimental. PUMA stripped our exclusivity because they wanted to sell more shoes elsewhere in the city!

Because of that, and because *Bikini Bandits* had crashed and burned, we closed up shop and literally converted the G*Mart retail space into the Sailor Jerry store.

But G*Mart was way ahead of its time, I now realize. It taught me how important it is for a brand to have a physical home. A brick-and-mortar place out of which the brand's culture, vibe, and energy can radiate.

We never would have done a Sailor Jerry retail store if we hadn't first done the G*Mart store.

In 2006, the Sailor Jerry store would move to a space below our offices when Gyro also moved from the shitty old bank building at Third and Walnut to our snazzy new office on Thirteenth and Sansom (paid for by Big Tobacco, no less).

By then, the Sailor Jerry brand was humming along. We had a place we could invite all these bands to drop by and visit, where we could do concerts in front of the store, just as we'd done with Phantom Planet at G*Mart.

I found full confirmation that G*Mart was ahead of its time when, starting in 2009, an artist collective from New Mexico began ripping me off with fake grocery store pop-ups. By 2021, they had officially opened their Omega Mart in Las Vegas. You have to buy $50 admission tickets to enter and look at their fake products such as Nut-Free Peanuts (instead of G*Mart's Deez Nuts). George R. R. Martin partially funds it and gets a lot of press. But it's glossy and arty. Not intentionally trashy, as G*Mart was.

Whatever.

I'm on to something else. Something that will be even more fun.

I've been thinking about applying for an art grant to open the Philadelphia Fart Museum.

I want to do this very elaborately and seriously. I would look at the historical writings of the founding fathers and put together what they ate, what their daily routines were, and then, based on that, mix a toxic brew of scents. So, based on our historical analysis of what, say, Ben Franklin ate and drank, this is what his farts would actually smell like.

In my grant proposal, I would have elaborate drawings and schematics of how museum guests would actually experience these smells. I'm already laughing about some uptight grant committee members reading my proposal.

Who knows, though? Maybe it would actually be funded.

Would you go?

YOU MAY LIVE IN A SHITTY PLACE, BUT IT'S YOUR SHITTY PLACE

Speaking of which, I'm always asked, "Why the fuck are you based in Philadelphia?"

Remember, this is the city that gave David Lynch such nightmares while he was a student at the Pennsylvania Academy of the Fine Arts that he created *Eraserhead.*

For me, though, Philadelphia isn't just a shitty place to live; it's the shitty place of my ancestors. I think it's important to know who you are and where you come from—it should really inform the basis of your creativity.

My dad's mother's side of the family first came to Philadelphia in 1708. My dad's dad's side first came to Philadelphia in 1812, escaping the Napoleonic Wars.

I am obsessed with the history of Philadelphia. I know every nook and cranny of this town. I have memorized every historical plaque. I am seriously the Cliff Clavin of Philadelphia history.

I regularly use my unreal knowledge of Philadelphia as an inspiration for my work. The problem with the major international cities is that they've been picked clean. Everyone has already used the same references, and all those are too familiar to people—even people who have never visited them.

I remember when Terry Gilliam shot *12 Monkeys* in Philadelphia in the mid-1990s, he said he was blown away by how, everywhere he looked, there was an amazing spot that had never appeared in any movie before. Try to find something new to shoot in Manhattan!

In Philadelphia, you're surrounded by decay, which keeps you humble and honest. It also keeps your creative output from being too influenced by the "now." The city is just so old.

I couldn't live in New York or LA or London. I'd be too distracted by the hubbub of high society and what everyone else in my field was doing. In those cities, at the big agencies, you're forced to develop design habits to impress your peers, to win dumb awards, not to enchant an audience.

That's one reason QCM hires only people who already live in Philadelphia. I don't want someone who has worked at the big agencies in New York. Someone who has an MBA from an Ivy League school. That person is already a lost cause. I want someone who still has imagination, whom I can hire and then train to tap into their brain.

If you live in New York, you can be too fearful of trying something new, of stepping off into the abyss, because you're afraid everyone will make fun of you for not fitting in. And then you'll lose your job. And then how will you pay for your $5,000-a-month studio apartment in Bushwick?

That's not the case for me here in shitty Philadelphia.

My younger brother recently told me that he thought Philadelphia had a "scuzz" like no other city.

(There's that word again.)

I agree.

And it's my greatest inspiration.

LESSON 2

BE LIKE BOWIE AND COMPLETELY
IGNORE WHAT EVERYONE ELSE IS DOING

Turn Off the TV, Get Off the Internet,
and Read Some Books

DAVID BOWIE, as I hinted earlier, has always been a major inspiration for me. Oddly, he was inspired by Philadelphia himself, having recorded his first live album, *David Live*, at the Tower Theater in Upper Darby during his 1974 Diamond Dogs tour and then, later that same year, recording his *Young Americans* album at the Sigma Sound Studios, about a half mile from my offices.

But it wasn't until I went to *David Bowie Is* at the Brooklyn Museum in 2018 that I realized why his work so resonated with me. This retrospective of the music legend's career displayed hundreds of artifacts from his life, everything from his stage costumes, props, and handwritten lyric sheets to his poetry, oil paintings, and other artwork—even his day-to-day possessions that allowed a British boy named David Robert Jones to become the immortal "David Bowie."

It was there, while wandering the exhibit, that I first learned that Bowie had traveled at all times with a retrofitted amplifier case packed with hundreds upon hundreds of books.

You see, Bowie was way ahead of the game. He was one of the original cultivators of curiosity. If his fellow musicians were reading mass-market paperbacks and fluffy magazines to pass the time while touring, Bowie consumed a broad library of esoteric books from the past.

The Iliad and Dante's *Inferno*. Dystopian novels by George Orwell and Anthony Burgess. Camus and Kafka. Poetry by Frank O'Hara and T. S. Eliot. *A Confederacy of Dunces*. He traveled with Éliphas Lévi's *Transcendental Magic: Its Doctrine and Ritual* and Julian Jaynes's *The Origin of Consciousness in the Breakdown of the Bicameral Mind*. He always had near him books on sexuality, politics, art, comedy, the quest for fame, and even the *Oxford English Dictionary*, which he once called a "really really long poem about everything."

And that, I truly believe, is how and why he became such a one-of-a-kind icon. Bowie was able to take these disparate, seemingly unrelated thoughts and rebuild them into his own innovations.

In one album, he's a bisexual alien in red boots; then he's a kook with crazy makeup; the next year, he's the Thin White Duke; then he's wearing an Alexander McQueen Union Jack waistcoat. Crazy! But it all makes sense. It all feels authentic to Bowie.

And lesser musicians couldn't rip him off even if they wanted to!

That's because a lesser musician wouldn't have spent years cultivating such deep and esoteric inspirations and then mashed them all together in a truly unique way, as Bowie did.

When I toured the Bowie exhibit, when I saw this cabinet of traveling books, I began to recall my first reading frenzy in Thailand that changed my life. I realized that what I was naturally doing with my own work was very similar to how Bowie created.

(I was likewise impressed by how meticulously Bowie chronicled all of his notes and ephemera, etc. It made me determined to hire a full-time archivist and historian, which I recently did.)

Bowie rarely talked about other musicians as a source of inspiration, and as you read this book, you'll notice that I don't talk a lot about other booze brands—whether to praise or deride them. I'm not trying to be cool, and I don't think my head is in the clouds when it comes to being aware of what else is going on in my industry.

But the fact is, I don't pay attention to what everybody else is doing.

Neither did Bowie.

When someone asks me, "Who else is doing something like that?"

I have to say, "I don't know."

"Who else is doing anything you like?"

"I'm not sure..."

I don't look at other booze brands because I don't really care what they do.

Fig. 25 Point Me Toward the Piñata

Like Bowie, I read old books. I watch old movies. I sort through arcane documents if I can get my hands on them (that's how Red Kamel came to be). I rummage through antique stores and strange shops (that's how the Hendrick's bottle came to be).

I don't waste time on the internet and social media because I believe being topical is the biggest mistake you can make when it comes to creation. Bowie realized that too. How do you differentiate yourself if you're "on-trend" like everyone else?

People are looking for enchantment, and you don't find that in trends. You find that in your own gut. So trust it!

It would have been easy for Bowie to scrap his plans and start dressing like a normal 1970s rocker after people mocked his androgynous space-age look. Of course, he didn't. Because he trusted his vision.

You're not supposed to be "of the moment."

Bowie was so not of the moment that many people thought he might truly be a Martian. Or a man from the future.

You're supposed to be so far out there that other people are trying to catch up to you. By the time they do, you're on to something new. Just like Bowie.

If you don't take anything else from this book, there's one thing I want you to remember, the one thing I want you to tell someone when they say, "Hey! What's that book you're reading about?"

Literally the crux of the book:

You need to unplug, stop opening Instagram and TikTok, and find unique sources of inspiration that aren't just for today but forever.

Like books.

Start cultivating those, and you'll already be ahead of most people.

You'll create something wholly unique and authentic to you.

And maybe the Brooklyn Museum will do a retrospective of your work in thirty years.

MY ALL-TIME FAVORITE BUSINESS AND MARKETING BOOKS

NONE.

I don't read them.

Like Bowie, I'm more interested in reading about a wide range of topics outside my supposed career.

So what do I read?

Books on robber barons, military generals, legendary inventors, scientists, the hermetic, the occult, old-time alchemy . . . and, always, epic stories of adventure. Long books, challenging books, out-of-print books.

Of course, you shouldn't just pick up my recommendations, or David Bowie's for that matter. You should read books not just because you think you will get profitable ideas from them but because they genuinely interest you.

Here's the cool thing, though.

The more you read stuff from the past and the more your interests go in all sorts of cool directions, the more you can make connections—or mash-ups, as I call them—between seemingly unrelated disciplines to create something completely new and original.

It doesn't only work in the world of art either.

I always think of Charles Darwin and Alfred Russel Wallace, the two men who independently came up with the theory of natural selection around the same time. Both had wide-ranging interests outside just nature and biology. They were explorers, geographers, geologists, and even mapmakers and illustrators in Wallace's case. Both were extremely well and widely read.

In fact, while cultivating their own curiosities, both had come across Thomas Robert Malthus's *An Essay on the Principle of Population*, an eighteenth-century economic tome on impending catastrophes with population growth. For both men, it was as if a lightbulb went off when they read Malthus. Darwin had simply picked up the book for some light "amusement" (as he explained later in his autobiography, *Recollections of the Development of My Mind and Character*), yet his search for an amusing read would ultimately change the world: "It at once struck me that under these circumstances favorable variations would tend to be preserved, and unfavorable ones to be destroyed. The result of this would be the formation of new species. Here, then, I had at last got a theory by which to work."

And this theory came about only because Darwin and Wallace might have been the only two men on the entire planet so curious as to have both observed exotic species while on their travels across the globe . . . and read Malthus for fun.

DON'T EMAIL ME: A DAY IN MY LIFE

PEOPLE ALWAYS WANT TO KNOW the minutiae of so-called successful people's day-to-day living. I guess that might be why I went to that Bowie exhibit. But it's not as if learning what time someone successful wakes up in the morning will revolutionize your life and career.

In my case, I think you'd benefit most by simply knowing how I think.

I believe creativity is a lifelong process. It requires deliberately exercising your mind. Building time into your daily schedule, every day, just to wander and think.

Cultivating curiosity—in yourself and then in others—needs to become your entire way of life.

This is my way.

I famously hate email.

I was still making people fax me, or even hand-deliver messages, until recently. There are just too many distractions out there that take away from deep work, and email is the worst of them all.

I will not look at email once I leave the office at 5 p.m. My thinking is that anything that's been emailed can wait until the morning, when I'm bright-eyed and bushy-tailed. If it's truly urgent, my assistant can always text me. I rarely get an urgent text from her, though.

This isn't some CEO power trip. By not looking at email past 5 p.m., I can shut off whatever craziness I may have experienced in the office during the day. Also, I'm not distracted in the evening and can pay attention to my family. (Yes, I recognize that this is a rare privilege I have as the boss, but I encourage my employees to push for no emails at night if they can too.)

I used to think I had very weird sleeping patterns, but then I learned—via what else? esoteric readings of medical texts and old diaries and even some Dickens—that the way I sleep is the way most people used to sleep before the advent of electricity and industrialism.

I go to bed at 8:30 p.m. most nights but then wake up at 2 a.m. and read for forty minutes to an hour. Then I go back to sleep and get up for the second time at 4:30 a.m.

(After fellow Philadelphian Kobe Bryant's death in 2020, it was reported that he too followed a routine of segmented sleep, believing it helped him get more work done during the day.)

When I wake up for the second time, at 4:30 a.m., I make a pot of coffee, put on some music, and get to work.

This is my GETTING-SHIT-DONE portion of the day.

I often think of R.E.M.'s "Finest Work Song":

Another chance has been engaged
To throw Thoreau and rearrange

I'm lucky to have a complete gym in my house, and I'm in it by 7 a.m. I won't bore you with my routine, but the gym also gives me time to digest podcasts as well as the *New York Times*, *Wall Street Journal*, and *Philadelphia Inquirer*. I still insist on having print editions delivered daily as well as a weekly stack of periodicals. I read them while I'm pedaling my decidedly non-Peloton exercise bike.

I am back working in my home office by 9 a.m., and this is when I take all the calls with my European clients. I also use this time to talk with my executive committee about HR stuff.

I go back to the gym from 11 a.m. to noon to do planks and watch shit on my iPad.

I then take a long walk to work at 1 p.m., listening en route to either my extensive music collection or audiobooks. I'm usually reading one or two books and listening to one or two books at the same time.

As I write this, I'm reading *The Invisible Rainbow: A History of Electricity and Life* by Arthur Firstenberg and *The Secret History of the World* by Mark Booth (a cool book about secret societies such as the Rosicrucians and the Alchemists) and listening to Ron Chernow's Pulitzer Prize–winning biography of George Washington.

I make myself devour books and esoterica every single day, like clockwork. No days off.

Cultivating curiosity is serious business.

I use this knowledge to fuel my work.

I've learned that the broader a base of deep esoteric knowledge and experiences you can pull from, the more you can find cosmic connections and create unique, cool shit. (Or maybe even discover natural selection, as Darwin did.)

I think of it as like having a giant box of Legos. Each Lego is a different piece of esoteric knowledge or facts or experience. Because they are Legos, you can always fit them together to build all sorts of weird shit.

It also helps that I pretty much have a photographic memory for just about everything I hear or read (except people's names, which drives my wife crazy). Back in the day, before the internet, when brainstorming with the team, I would always blow people's minds by saying, "There's a book in our library . . . third shelf down . . . if you look at page 135, there is a picture of *this* . . . and if we take *that* . . . and mix it with *this* . . . then we might have *something*."

Of course, the need for that talent has declined a bit with the internet. Still, you need to know where to look for stuff, and what to look for in the first place, so you still have to build a deep set of knowledge to begin with.

I insist on coming to the office every day. I need the routine.

I want my employees to see me and think, If this guy can come in every day, I can too.

I get to the office and have in-person creative meetings in some form from 2 to 5 p.m.

I leave at exactly 5 p.m. and again take a long walk home, again listening to audiobooks ... or just letting my mind wander.

I walk between seven and ten miles a day. Walking is superimportant to my creative process. It's how I think. And there's a great flaneur tradition among many innovators such as Darwin, Einstein, Thoreau ("Me thinks that the moment my legs begin to move, my thoughts begin to flow"), and even Steve Jobs, all of whom used walks to inspire thought.

If I have a good thought on my walk, I'll email myself a nugget of the idea. I find that if I don't send myself emails, I'll forget the idea by the time I get home. So I may not email with other people all that much, but I email myself constantly.

When I wander into neighborhoods I've never explored before, I'll stop and read all the historical plaques on buildings and statues and monuments. Every single one.

My family eats promptly at 6:30 p.m. My wife is an amazing cook. We all sit down and eat together every single night. It's mandatory.

In the summers, we go live on our farm in New Hampshire for three months. We have 1996 AOL dial-up-quality internet speeds and no Wi-Fi, so I'm barely able to even use it. Which is great. We have no Netflix or any streaming services either because the internet is too slow to handle them.

That means I can only read physical books and occasionally watch old movies. We have a collection of more than five hundred DVDS at the house, a lot of obscure classics from the 1930s and '40s. Even my son has learned to love old cinema.

This forced unplugging in New Hampshire is key to my creativity, and I always feel superproductive in the summer while everyone else is goofing around at the beach.

I refuse to travel for business anymore. It's a waste of time.

When we vacation as a family, though, our trips are always tied to historical curiosity and adventure: hiking the Andes, exploring French Polynesia—we even went to a wedding in Transylvania once.

Our kids have been everywhere and seen everything, and they will eat anything anywhere we go on the planet. I hope that we have done a good job cultivating their own curiosity. I'm pretty sure we have. In fact, I know we have because my daughter chose to go to school at St. John's College in Annapolis, the third-oldest college in America and one of the most unique. There you study ancient Greek and read stuff like Aristotle and Thucydides (in Greek) before delving fully into the Western canon, Homer and Ovid, and learning astronomy and math like some nineteenth-century scholar, reading literal source materials written by Copernicus and Einstein. The goal isn't to train you for a vocation, as at most universities these days, but to train you to be thoughtful. The *New York Times* called it "The Most Contrarian College in America," and that was a compliment.

I think more people would benefit from that kind of contrarian learning. It's not antiquated, as people believe.

All this deep thinking, boundless curiosity, intellectual routine, and rigor in your life open your third eye. They increase your perception.

This approach adds mysticism to everything you create by connecting you to the past. That's where all the good ideas are hiding.

Fig. 26 Don't Let the Bed Bugs Bite

Fig. 27 Old Fuss and Feathers

LESSON 3
HOW DELVING INTO THE PAST
CAN REVIVE THE PRESENT

OKAY, you just walked seven to ten miles, you're home, you're sweaty, and you're thinking, "Grasse! Nothing happened. How do long walks actually lead to me producing stuff in the real world?"

I'll tell you my process.

When I was walking home from work today listening to Chernow's *Washington*, the narrator began talking about a conflict between Britain and Spain that lasted nearly a decade in the mid-1700s. It was fought mainly in New Granada and the West Indies in the Caribbean Sea and featured one of the largest fleets ever gathered, led by Lawrence Washington, the future president's older half-brother.

I perked up when I heard what this conflict was called: the War of Jenkins' Ear.

The War of Jenkins' Ear!

I quit walking, paused the audiobook, and immediately sent an email to myself. Because, you have to admit, that is a great fucking name!

And the name becomes more interesting when you see that it refers to Robert Jenkins, a captain of a British merchant ship whose ear was cut off by Spanish coast guards in 1731 when they boarded his ship in a time of peace, the impetus for the conflict to come.

The War of Jenkins' Ear.

Could it be used for an American whiskey or a Spanish gin or maybe a West Indies rum?

What if it was a spirit you couldn't just smell and taste but could also hear? Would that be possible?

This is how I'm always thinking.

Just hearing that cool name has my mind activated, engaged.

I don't know if I'll ever use the War of Jenkins' Ear, if it'll ever inspire the creation of something you will one day see on a liquor store shelf. But maybe I'll sit down with Jamie Oakes, our master distiller, and Matt Power, our biochemist mad scientist, and we'll brainstorm about what this name could become.

A gin that uses some animals' ears as a botanical?

Forget the worm in a bottle of mezcal; how about a floating ear?

Maybe I'll never use the name, and I'll pass it along to some heavy-metal band I run into one day to use instead.

Take it—it's yours.

I have an endless supply because the past is chock-full of these inspirations. That's my point.

You just have to GET OFF FUCKING SOCIAL MEDIA AND STOP BINGEING THE LATEST TV SHOWS TO FIND THEM.

Read challenging books, watch obscure foreign films, listen to esoteric podcasts.

Here's another great name I came across recently: Old Fuss & Feathers.

That's what Winfield Scott, the legendary army general of War of 1812 fame, was known as.

Old Fuss & Feathers.

Another great fucking name!

Another great place to start brainstorming a potential brand from.

One more: Royal Gift.

Sounds unassuming, but that's the name George Washington gave the Zamorano-Leonés donkey that King Charles III of Spain sent him in November 1784. Royal Gift was one prized jackass. So let's use that name for an exceedingly rare whiskey we'll release.

I love discovering this obscure shit, and I could go on forever. In fact, we have a file of hundreds if not thousands of possible brand names just sitting around waiting for us to strike, waiting for us to find a cool way to use them.

You're probably not going to find stuff like this in a Netflix documentary.

Watch the same Netflix documentaries as everyone else, and you end up making a product based on a lame *Tiger King* reference that'll be outdated by the time it's on the shelf.

But if you make sure you consume materials that no one else is consuming, you might learn about things that are so fucking weird, no one else will know about them—and then! And then—this is key—you might be inspired to create something that will eventually break through because it'll make everyone say, "Where the hell did you get that name?"

"What is it from?"

"What does it mean?"

And then you'll mystify people with your source material.

(Yes, these days there are no truly original ideas. Every idea comes from somewhere, is inspired by something.)

You're building your onion.

All around poor Jenkins's severed ear.

Fig. 28 Ten Gallon Hat

★ THE MAGICAL INGREDIENT ★

GOOD AND DIFFERENTIATED LIQUID

What It All Comes Down To

I HOPE YOU DON'T THINK at this point that my successes in business are just around finding crazy names in old books.

Of course, you also need great liquid! That is to say, great *product*, whatever that might be.

This seems self-evident.

But, as we all know, taste is subjective.

For instance, I'm surprisingly easy to please drinks-wise. I like lager beer and neat spirits, never cocktails. (And I pretty much exclusively drink my own products these days, so take that for what it's worth.)

So when I say the first magical ingredient for a great booze brand is always going to be good liquid, what I really mean is that you need liquid that has a point of difference that is easy for consumers to understand.

For instance, Sailor Jerry isn't going to win some rum connoisseur's tasting panel, but that's not its point. It's simply meant to be a boozier Captain Morgan. It's 92 proof versus a puny 70 proof, and for only about a dollar more.

That's not genius by any means, but the product isn't positioned for people who sniff and sip and jot down tasting notes in tiny Moleskines and really consider their alcohol.

It's for people who want to have a good time partying at home with spiced rum.

With Hendrick's Gin, on the other hand, I remember sitting in an early meeting, talking about what the signature drink call would be for Hendrick's. A Hendrick's Tonic and . . .

Cucumber!

Mind you, I had literally just learned how gin was made ten minutes before, how this ancient Carter-Head still had a gin basket that you could put any botanical you wanted into.

So why not cucumbers?

At the time, it seemed as if no one really liked gin anyway. At least, not the way they do nowadays. Back then, it was still seen as something grannies drank at the country club.

That was why I thought we should specifically create a gin for non-gin drinkers.

And Lesley Gracie came up with something wonderful.

Floral, cucumber-y, easy-drinking. Gin that works for a non-gin drinker.

That's the differentiation in the liquid.

And it worked!

Since there were way more non-gin drinkers than gin drinkers, it sold incredibly well. Even lightweights who had been drinking the cupcake-flavored vodka of the era loved Hendrick's.

Again, I'm not a distilling genius. My involvement in creating a spirit is that simple: Here's an idea. Can it be made?

(And if it can, let's build an entire brand world to support it.)

It doesn't even need to be the craziest idea in the world.

With Tamworth's Chocorua Rye Whiskey, I wanted a classic, old-school American, East Coast rye whiskey. When my distillery came back with one that had a mash bill that was 100 percent rye, something that is almost never done, I knew our liquid had that distinctive story. (Even the ubiquitously sourced rye that many "fake" craft distilleries use is only 95 percent rye.)

Likewise, Tamworth's Apple Brandy VSOP was spawned by me asking, "Why is there no legit apple brandy category in America?" Meanwhile, cognac—grape brandy from France—is, of course, a massive luxury category.

Tamworth initially had an apple brandy called Old Hampshire. It was delicious, using heirloom apples from a New Hampshire family farm. It did okay sales-wise, but nothing special. That's annoying because apple brandy is very expensive to make, as you need to ferment a shit-ton of apples for each batch.

So I decided to let that massive expense work for us. I thought, Cognac is famously expensive. And famously classy. Cognac also has that abbreviated labeling system most Americans probably don't understand.

VS. XO. VSOP.

Who knows what the hell that means? Americans don't. We just know it means it's fancy.

I wondered if we could use a designation like that on American apple brandy. Cognac may be a geographically protected product, but they don't own any of the designations.

Voilà!

Tamworth Garden Apple Brandy VSOP.

It stands for Very Superior Old Pale and means the brandy is at least four years old. It's a beautiful product, and very traditional, even down to the packaging. But with that VSOP designation, we're giving our liquid a distinction befitting how good it is. Despite the high price, it immediately started selling like gangbusters. *Esquire* even cited it as one of the best new spirits in the country.

My point is that you need to give your liquid—or whatever thing you're trying to sell—a damn angle.

No one wants another dry gin, no matter how delicious.

No one needs another bourbon, no matter how tasty.

When I worked on PUMA, we used to always say, "Nobody wants vanilla from PUMA."

If you wanted vanilla, you could get it from Nike or Adidas or Reebok or certainly New Balance.

Even today, a lot of aspiring whiskey companies come to me, excited: "We've acquired some fantastic liquid from MGP, and we have an idea for a new brand! Can you help us?"

MGP, or Midwest Grain Products, is, of course, the big factory in Indiana where hundreds of whiskey companies source that aforementioned 95 percent rye liquid. It's great stuff, but it's the same stuff everyone else has been bottling for over a decade.

So I'll tell them flat out, I don't care what your story is; if you're using MGP, it's just going to be another bourbon.

So you've got a long, expensive slog in front of you.

Because if you don't have a differentiated product, it's going to take a lot of time, money, and effort to make that damn thing stick in the consciousness.

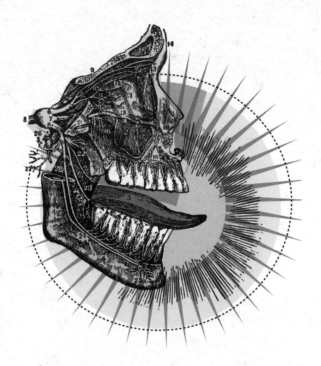

GOOD TASTE IS <u>NOT</u> SUBJECTIVE

I JUST TOLD YOU that taste is subjective. True.

But *good* taste certainly isn't.

When I say this, it absolutely drives people crazy—it makes them seriously annoyed!

Someone is already penning a rebuttal to this very chapter, I'd imagine! But it's true.

The reason people think good taste is subjective is that they think taste is immutable. They think that whatever they naturally enjoy watching or reading or eating or drinking is *their* good taste, and who are you to judge?

In their mind, to say someone has bad taste is to insult who they inherently are—no different than making fun of them for being short or blond.

But here's the thing: No one is born with good taste. Just like creativity and curiosity, good taste is something you cultivate through years of learning, research, and experience.

Good taste is just cultural literacy. The more literate you are, the better taste you are able to have.

I'll sometimes hear young people say something like this after they just saw *Citizen Kane* for the first time: "This is not the greatest film of all time! It's sooo boring." It's a cool, provocative thing to say, no different than claiming *Moby Dick* sucks or a Michelin-starred restaurant is overrated.

They're wrong, of course.

They just don't know any better.

How can they accurately judge *Citizen Kane* if they don't know about William Randolph Hearst, the media landscape of the early twentieth century, and the hullabaloo surrounding the picture's release in 1941? If they don't know how audacious Orson Welles's directing was for the time, how cinematographer Gregg Toland's visual mastery completely changed the industry? If they don't know all the future filmmakers and films it would inspire, the references it would spawn in everything from François Truffaut's *Day for Night* to *Raiders of the Lost Ark* to even *The Simpsons*, the White Stripes, and Donald Trump's presidential campaign?

How can they judge it if they haven't watched it a half-dozen times to see all the little secrets hidden on the screen, the onion that continues to unravel the more you study it?

How can they fully judge *Citizen Kane*'s greatness if they're too young to have ever loved, to have ever lost, to have ever massively succeeded or embarrassingly failed?

I'm not saying that something can be judged a masterpiece, or even "good," only if you're an expert on the subject. But it's sheer arrogance to think you can spend all day goofing around on TikTok and watching crappy Netflix shows and then easily dismiss something that everyone throughout history has deemed a masterpiece.

Of course, they could be right. I'm certainly not saying to never take down sacred cows. *Citizen Kane* might be overrated, *Moby Dick* might suck, Noma might be no better than Burger King.

But here's my assignment for you.

If you ever encounter something that critics and scholars agree is great and then try it and don't like it, don't immediately assume that your taste is the taste that is actually correct. Instead, do the work to understand why the cognoscenti revere something.

Understanding and accepting what is good taste is a choice. Becoming culturally literate is the only way to acquire good taste.

There's a reason that aesthetics was such a major branch of philosophy. Just like ethics or science or even sporting skills, the ancient Greeks knew that there was a correct answer, a better choice. Some things are beautiful, some things are brilliant, some runners are faster than others, some things are delicious . . . and many other things are not.

The deeper your esoteric knowledge, the more you know what is good, and the more sources you have to pull from, the better your own taste becomes. It's pretty much that simple.

It's what happened to me. My brands are built on aesthetic mash-ups of the esoteric cultural and historical things I know about only because I've cultivated my curiosity for years. It's why each brand's layers of the onion work together so well.

For us at QCM, aesthetics is a goal unto itself.

And it's why we so value good taste.

Especially in my world, the spirits world, people will say you can't judge a book by its cover. In other words: great bourbon *could* have a shitty label.

I disagree.

Sort of.

Yes, great bourbon could have a shitty label as long as the label is authentically shitty or even intentionally shitty (like our Sailor Jerry example).

But if it truly has a shitty label?

Well, then, it's inherently not a great bourbon.

SO YOU REFUSE TO LISTEN TO ME AND WANNA CREATE YET ANOTHER SOURCED BOURBON BRAND?

(That Is Not What This Book Is For)

MAYBE YOU BOUGHT THIS BOOK because you've recently come up with some get-rich-quick scheme to source some whiskey and become a booze maven yourself.

This chapter is for you, to urge you to get your deposit back on those barrels you just bought.

A few years ago, William Grant & Sons again came to me. They wanted an American whiskey in their portfolio.

"And we don't want to distill it ourselves!" they told me.

Gee, but sourcing a whiskey is boring, I told them. Everyone already does that. They weren't deterred.

I decided to see this as a challenge. With this assignment, they gave me an opportunity to take something that is generally seen as boring and lazy and find a way to make it still interesting.

First, I asked myself, what can we do that's unique in the bourbon category?

WGS, of course, has a longtime history of Scottish blending experience—so I started there and began to wonder whether they could take that thing they are uniquely good at and apply it to American bourbon. Of course, that would raise another issue, as the term "blended whiskey" has a negative connotation in American whiskey parlance, generally meaning a cheap whiskey combined with grain alcohol and other crap to make a light, economical, and bottom-shelf product.

But technically, it didn't *have* to mean that.

By this point in time, a decade or so into the "craft" whiskey movement, we'd already seen what sophisticated American blending could look like. There's the famous case of High West Distilling out of Park City, Utah. David Perkins, their founder, had done some really intriguing stuff like blending a sourced rye whiskey with a sourced bourbon to create a product fittingly called Bourye. He'd also blended a sourced bourbon with a smoky single malt from Scotland for something called Campfire. Really cool stuff.

I'd also always liked the way craft breweries come up with wacky names for their beers. Speedway Stout. Horny Devil. Pliny the Elder. They've never been bound by the formal (and boring) naming conventions that the whiskey industry seems to be stuck with. Wild Turkey 101. Weller 12. Jim Beam White Label. Johnnie Walker Black.

Boring.

I wanted to give this bourbon a name that would be completely different, completely out of place, completely fucking crazy compared to everything on the shelf beside it, all the "Olds" and "Rares" and "Whites" and "Blacks."

One of my writers suggested a name: Fistful of Bourbon.

I liked it!

And it got my creative juices flowing . . .

Now, a fistful—that would be five fingers. Hmmm. I wondered . . . could they blend five sourced bourbons together from five different places? A literal fistful of bourbon?

They could, and WGS sent their wunderkind master blender Kelsey McKechnie to the United States to source bourbon from five different distilleries throughout the country, in Kentucky, Tennessee, Indiana, and New York. She then put together a beautiful, complex, "smooth as hell" blend.

The label would evoke that craft beer vibe—bright, colorful, a little cartoonish—and mash the marketing up with, no surprise, what the name was meant to evoke: *Fistful of Dollars*, the cult 1964 spaghetti Western starring Clint Eastwood and directed by the Italian master Sergio Leone.

Our designer did a first-draft rough design for the packaging, essentially evoking that modern craft beer aesthetic combined with a 1960s spaghetti Western movie poster. WGS accidentally got their hands on it before we were finished and sent it out for testing. Something I hate, but it didn't matter. It ended up getting the highest marks of any label design they'd ever focus-grouped.

Fig. 29 Pappy Van Stinkle

Of course—and this is the biggest challenge, I tell prospective booze brands—it's really damn hard to talk people into buying a pricey bottle of spirits they've never heard of before.

Why would anyone pay $50 for Bourbon X when they already know they like Evan Williams and it's only $20 a bottle? (For what it's worth, we got Fistful to market at just $23 a bottle.)

We knew that would be a challenge here. So we designed Fistful of Bourbon to overcome that problem. This was a product that was devised for retail, with its eye-popping label, a name you kind of knew from pop culture, and a compelling brand story.

Unfortunately, if Sailor Jerry showed my good fortune come launch time, Fistful of Bourbon would force me to deal with bad luck: It launched during the absolute height of the COVID-19 pandemic.

A time when many businesses were closed, and even those liquor stores that were open weren't allowing people to stroll in and wander the aisles looking at new things. I had planned on that being our bread and butter, with a brand ambassador posted in various stores, telling shoppers the brand's origin story and offering samples of the product.

"It's a blend of five bourbons. A fistful. Here, have a finger . . ."

Instead, the pandemic placed a huge roadblock in our path, forcing us to get even more creative in our marketing. For example, we hired Paul Briganti, who does all the viral filmed pieces for *SNL*, to do a series of Fistful of Bourbon movie trailers, all spoofing life at a Wild West saloon. We also did a very stunty search to find an official "SpokesFist" for the brand—$100,000 to the right fist. We got a ton of entries and a ton of press. Further bolstered by an influencer campaign, we landed hundreds of five-star reviews on Drizly and had boffo online sales there as well.

So, despite the shitstorm of 2020, despite all the bad luck and obstacles thrown in our launch path, Fistful of Bourbon became a huge success. Which kind of proves the point of this entire book: If you have great liquid, a great story, and great packaging, it will work every time.

Even if the entire world can't leave their house for a year.

'GANSETT, KNUCKLEHEAD MARKETING, AND COMING AHEAD ON A SUCKER DEAL

IN 2008, I fully sold the Sailor Jerry intellectual property to WGS and now had a little extra money. I was looking to invest it. My old PUMA pal Tony Bertone told me I should meet with him and Mark Hellendrung, the former president of Nantucket Nectars. They had just acquired, from Pabst, the brand name to an old and, by then, defunct Rhode Island brewery called Narragansett.

As I recall, Pabst sold the brand to Mark for some ridiculously low sum, but it was what we call a sucker deal. Apparently it was written into their contract that if they didn't sell an incredibly high number of barrels of beer within the next five years, then the brand name would revert to Pabst.

So Mark and his other investors were set to do all the hard fucking work to revive a brand, to get it up and running again, with Pabst knowing full well they could never possibly reach that number of barrels sold so quickly. Thus, they'd then lose that new, emerging brand right back to Pabst.

I always like a challenge, and I particularly liked the potential for Narragansett, so I agreed to get on board.

The three of us met at Legal Seafood in Boston one afternoon for a boozy lunch. We sat there for hours, Tony, Mark, and I, mapping out the entire brand strategy.

Cheap yellow lager is a tough sell in America because you can never be cheaper than Bud, Miller, or Coors. A lot of it tastes the same, so differentiating your liquid is nearly impossible too.

So I figured we'd need to enchant New Englanders with the idea of a local brew. (It had, in fact, once been the best-selling beer in New England.) We'd need to get people to have pride in this local lager over the mass-market swill coming from some faceless corporate factory in Colorado, Milwaukee, or St. Louis.

But that's easier said than done.

We quickly realized what our biggest struggle was going to be.

How were we going to position Narragansett as a local Rhode Island brand when, at least to start, we would need to contract the beer brewing to Genesee Brewery in Rochester, New York?

Fuck.

How do you fix a problem like that?

In this case, I simply decided we should lean into it and admit what we were doing.

We launched a whole campaign called "Drink Your Part."

The gist was, every 'Gansett you bought was another brick for the brewery we would one day build in Pawtucket. And if you (meaning the Rhode Island locals) didn't drink enough beer over the next several years, then we wouldn't be able to build a local brewery.

"So drink your part!" we said.

We were very transparent. We were just some young guys trying to revive a legendary brand.

I think this honest strategy really built up a lot of goodwill and local equity among Rhode Island beer drinkers. Indeed, everyone wanted to drink their part.

It also helped that Mark went to great lengths to make the beer taste better. Back in the late 1970s, after a leveraged buyout specialist obtained majority control of the brand and began cutting costs, the beer's quality declined so much that it earned the nickname "Nasty 'Gansett." Wanting to repair that image, Mark found the former brewmaster, Bill Anderson, then in his seventies, who knew the original recipe. He helped recreate its original flavor and returned the beer to its former glory. It quickly became the highest-rated American lager on *Beer Advocate*.

So now, just as with Sailor Jerry, we had a point of difference with our liquid. For just a few cents more than BudMillerCoors, you could have a classic American lager, locally made (well . . . soon enough), that didn't taste like shit.

We also employed what I call "Knucklehead Marketing."

That's when you intentionally try to make something so bad that it's good, a bit similar to our Sailor Jerry "ugly on purpose" design strategy.

We started calling Mark "Chief Gansett" in homage to this crazy old cartoon character that no less than Theodor Geisel (aka Dr. Seuss) himself had created for the brand back in the 1930s.

We added other characters to the brand universe in these sort of Disneyland-from-hell-type costumes.

Tall Boy was a giant can of beer.

Clammy was a giant clam, owing to Pawtucket's longtime clamming heritage.

Then there was the Beer Fairy, a big dude with fairy wings, simple as that.

We were building a beer wack pack in a way, like a brewery version of Howard Stern's oddest cast members.

This was my Onion Method at its finest.

Since Narragansett's brand mysticism was so corny, it became obvious that it was authentic and not some big, slick marketing campaign funded by millions of dollars. Then I began using my skills at pranks to get press. We would do these crazy stunts. We had nothing to lose.

Back then, the Rhode Island School of Design had a mascot called Scrotie, a student dressed in a literal penis costume. So we arranged to have Scrotie and

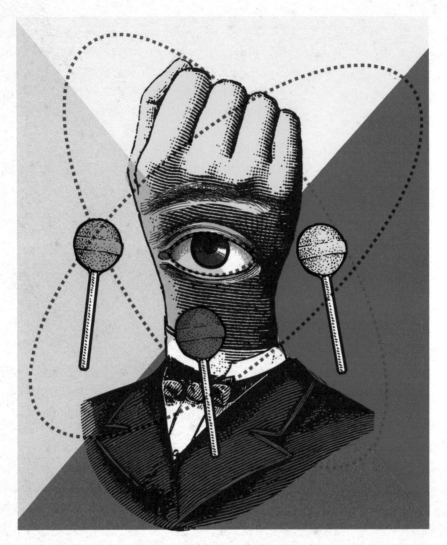

Fig. 30 Sweeter Than Candy on a Stick

Clammy get into a fight during one of the school's hockey matches. The college kids loved it and drank a shitload of our beer.

Eventually we started doing limited can drops, creative grenades that built on what I'd learned during my time with PUMA.

We did collaborations with Del's Lemonade and Autocrat Coffee Syrup, two beloved Rhode Island institutions, producing a shandy and milk stout, respectively. Those two brands are so sacred to locals that it raised us in their esteem.

We also released a 1975 throwback can to honor the thirty-fifth anniversary of *Jaws* in 2010, reviving the design of the exact 'Gansett can Robert "Captain Quint" Shaw famously crushed in the Steven Spielberg blockbuster. (Even this had authenticity: Spielberg had apparently interviewed Martha's Vineyard fishermen to see what they actually drank, and their answer was 'Gansett.)

We likewise launched a whole series of beers to honor horror writer and Providence native H. P. Lovecraft, himself a master of the Onion Method, with can designs and beer names inspired by his work. To this day, each new Lovecraft 'Gansett release is a huge hit.

And, yes, just as with Sailor Jerry, we got a little lucky too.

In New York City at the time, our distributor, Union in Brooklyn, just happened to be looking for a PBR killer. PBR had been *the* hipster beer du jour in downtown Manhattan and Brooklyn for most of the aughts, but it was now ripe for being overthrown. We surfed the perfect wave that Union created for us and replaced PBR in many of the city's coolest bars.

And do I even need to tell you? Of course, we hit that sucker number Pabst had set for us.

Far surpassed the number, in fact.

Today, Narragansett is the thirtieth largest brewery in America among more than eight thousand contenders.

And the Pawtucket brewery opened in the summer of 2021.

Everyone had indeed drunk their part.

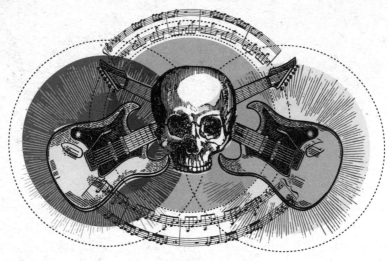

LESSON 4

YOU NEED TO THINK LIKE FOUR UNEDUCATED GUYS IN A GARAGE

*Teddy Bears, Tolkien, Two Drummers,
and Singing Like Donald Duck*

As with Rhode Islanders and their love for 'Gansett, it's pretty easy to see that people thirst for authentic stuff (no pun intended). They can sense when it's actually the real deal, so you can't lie to them. And sometimes, the most legitimate way to be real is just following your inspiration wherever it leads you, even if you have no idea where you're headed.

Something like Red Kamel is an amazing example. By accident, we were able to take an obscure brand from one hundred years ago, spelled differently from the main brand, with a color scheme that didn't make any sense—and which some people even thought was communist!—and turn it into a sensation.

In fact, that was exactly why it grabbed smokers' fascination and interest. It was intriguing, shrouded in mystery, and seemed to carry the weight of some unknown history. They didn't know what it was and had never seen such a thing.

My wife, who is nine years younger than I, told me she had Red Kamel ads all over her dorm room walls at Occidental College. She thought it was cool. To her, it was no different than hanging up posters for rock bands or cool fashion brands of the time such as Diesel.

With Red Kamel, I had inadvertently stumbled upon this thing about creativity:

It doesn't need to make sense!

In fact, sometimes the more fucked up something is, the more different it is, the more it *doesn't* add up ... the better.

In time, I also began to realize that this revelation could explain the way a rock band inherently comes up with stuff too, and maybe Quaker City Mercantile should start thinking more like rock bands.

What's the aesthetic of Led Zeppelin?

It's something like Mississippi blues meets heavy metal meets ... J. R. R. Tolkien?

That doesn't make any sense!

If someone told you they were starting a band around that concept, you'd tell them to keep their day job.

Or the Grateful Dead. Teddy bears and skulls and roses and pot and songs that never fucking end. But it somehow comes together to form something unique, and then a sensation.

Seriously, think about how stupid Rush sounds when I just write it down. They're like a mixture of sci-fi plus Ayn Rand, and it's just a trio of Canadians with Geddy Lee singing like Donald Duck just swallowed helium. It's so weird that it's completely unique to them. You hear a Rush song on the radio, and you instantly know who it is, even if you've never heard that particular song before.

That's the beautiful naivete of a rock band.

They're not professionals.

They certainly don't have MBAs.

They're not focus group tested.

They're not trying to impress their colleagues on Madison Avenue.

They're usually just a few high school friends who came together in a garage and did whatever they thought was cool.

I'll repeat: Whatever *they* thought was cool.

And that creates this very authentic presence that makes no sense yet resonates with people because it comes off as an earnest creation that is unique and truly their own.

Thus, tribes form around these bands because fans can sense that earnestness and authenticity.

Today, with every new brand I create, I try to think of it as a garage band starting out.

If you think of your brand as just a brand—you end up with Velveeta. Boring.

More than filmmakers, more than novelists (who, even at their most experimental, tend to use linear storytelling methods), bands just throw shit together in a weird way and make it work.

It's something that simply can't be replicated by a big corporation in a lab.

Back in the early days, whenever we'd get a new client, often from these bigger companies, they'd spend a lot of time talking to us about their "trend analysis." They'd have all these businesspeople come in and tell me about their quantitative testing and qualitative testing and other buzzwords. They'd have demographic research from focus groups and pages of spreadsheets. And loads of consultants who would tell me "what's hot" at that very second in time.

I'd always think, Who cares what's hot right now? It won't be hot by the time we get the brand to market!

In fact, I don't care about the current zeitgeist at all. I purposely put blinders on myself so that I don't really notice it.

Look again at that Brooklyn small-batch, handcrafted, whatever-the-fuck thing that started about a decade ago. Gourmet mayonnaise and gluten-free ice-cream sandwiches and $25 bottles of artisan hot sauce. Everyone seemed to care only about how cool they could make the label look, as opposed to creating a unique story. Even as it was occurring, I remember thinking, My god, all this shit looks the same—there are no brands there!

PART II • MY BOOZE LIFE

Everybody was riffing off the same aesthetic. It looks alright technically, but when you dig down deep under the surface, there's no *brand* to those brands. No story. It's just a very generic vibe. Those brands eventually fade away.

(What *was* the name of that $25 artisan hot sauce?)

There's no meaning behind them, so when the style changes, they are left with nothing.

But Hendrick's hasn't gone out of style. And Led Zeppelin has never gone out of style because they weren't trying to be trendy when they started out, and they certainly were not trying to evoke the moment they lived in. They were just being themselves.

Or at least the version of themselves when they were a bunch of dumb kids sitting around a basement in London jamming.

Fig. 31 Charles Atlas Walks Into a Bar

SELF-ESTEEM FOR BIG BRANDS: HIGH LIFE, PILSNER URQUELL, AND GUINNESS

NARRAGANSETT TAUGHT ME that it takes serious skills to market "yellow" beer.

Selling beer in America used to be all about massive ad budgets and silly jingles and Spuds MacKenzie. No one talked about what the beer actually tasted like aside from maybe telling you it "Tastes Great" (and is "Less Filling").

But then craft beer came along and completely changed the game, using exotic hops, wild yeasts, and esoteric ingredients. This was beer absolutely jam-packed with a differentiation of flavor, and it was easy to market it that way.

So if you are a global "yellow beer" brand, what do you do? Well, you call the guy (and his team) who made 'Gansett unexpectedly successful, a yellow beer exploding in this brave new world of IPAs and sour ales.

Of course, these global macrobrands do tend to have one thing over the craft upstarts: layers of stories and history that, in the right hands, could become as golden a marketing tool as those exotic hops and wild yeasts.

Most of these brands just hadn't *told* their stories in a long while.

I realized it would be QCM's job to be a sort of self-esteem coach for them. To delve into their brand's past and look for clues to what they are all about, what they could still be proud of. I felt that it was our job with these vintage beer brands to distill their essence and harness it for modern times.

I knew if we leaned on a brand as simply being old as shit, people would just look at it like it's old as shit.

I thought, instead, we should do mash-ups of these brands' best assets throughout their storied histories and then regurgitate them in a way that a new consumer would find intriguing.

★

PILSNER URQUELL

SABMILLER, WHICH OWNED the famous Czech pilsner at the time, came to us and said, "What can you do to fix this brand?"

Well, what's the problem?

The problem was, they couldn't ship it anywhere—it would immediately skunk.

They didn't need a fucking lab team to know why this was occurring. It was simply because it was bottled in green glass, which couldn't protect the liquid from UV light, which causes iso-alpha acids in the hops to break down and emit the putrid, skunk-like smell.

It seemed like a simple solution.

"Why do you put it in green glass?" I wondered.

"Because we always have," they responded.

That's never a good reason, but brands love to stick with what they've always done, and you'll rarely convince them otherwise.

So my team did some research in the SABMiller archives—and found that "we always have" wasn't even true!

Pilsner Urquell started bottling in green glass only after World War II because (A) it was cheaper than brown glass, which had been needed for the war effort, and (B) they wanted to emulate Heineken, which was red-hot at the time and which they clearly still envied.

Doing something just because Heineken does it was an even worse reason to do something! Pilsner Urquell is such a different beast. Pilsner Urquell is literally the original pilsner. It's still made in the city of Plzeň.

So we developed a line, "Keepers of the Craft," saying that Pilsner Urquell was the original craft beer. We would use their longtime heritage to reinforce this fact.

We began releasing cans (impossible to skunk) with vintage labels. I took a trip to Prague and Plzeň and saw that the beer was treated much more reverently than it is in America. (I was over there for just a few days, and I think I drank more beer that week than I had in the previous year combined.)

Some bars in the country even serve unpasteurized, less-than-forty-eight-hours-old Pilsner Urquell from giant see-through tanks underneath the bar. They call it *Tankovna* beer, and it's incredible.

I thought, Why not build these tank bars all across Europe?

We did, and they were a sensation. The brand exploded, again claiming its rightful place on the world's pilsner throne.

★

MILLER HIGH LIFE

NOW, THIS BRAND WAS WELL AWARE that they were a cult favorite with bartenders and hipsters and hipster bartenders—but Miller was doing the stupidest thing possible with it. They were marketing directly to those people, trying to reflect them in the actual advertising with scraggly, bearded dudes ranting to the camera in black-and-white.

To me, it was embarrassing.

'Gansett had similarly become a hipster favorite, but we never, ever did ads with hipsters in them. "Hey, cool people, this brand is for you!" To me, this is What Not to Do 101.

Miller asked me to come to a meeting, and I told them, "This is a classic car you have. And what do you do with a classic car? You restore it."

My wife, Sonia, told me she thought High Life was like Hellmann's mayonnaise and Heinz ketchup. I know that sounds crazy, if not insulting, but what she meant was that Hellmann's and Heinz are sold in the supermarket. They are mass produced. They aren't "craft."

But they are the gold standard.

I liked that idea.

Nobody wants fucking craft ketchup. They want Heinz! We all have that ingrained memory of its classic flavor. Heinz simply is what ketchup is supposed to taste like.

Miller High Life loved this idea, and we set out to restore the brand to its rightful place as a true classic. This started with totally redoing their packaging, painstakingly restoring the beer like the classic car it was.

Everyone already knows their marketing slogan, "The Champagne of Beers." In a way, what they had been doing was working against that. Drinkers in dive bars had started to toast to "The Champagne of Beers" ironically. It had become a joke to many Americans.

We spent a lot of time investigating why it was ever called the Champagne of Beers in the first place. First, it was made with a unique yeast that gives Miller High Life its signature tiny bubbles and effervescence.

More notable is its sloping-shouldered bottle design. When it was first introduced in 1903, most places were still serving beer in a dirty glass at the saloon. Or a literal bucket to go. For a beer to be sold in a clear glass—so that you could actually see those tiny bubbles!—with a gold foil wrapping, now, that was classy!

I started looking at High Life through that lens and asking myself, When did this brand become a joke? When did this brand become something people only drank ironically?

Thus, my goal was to dust it off, shine it up, and not talk about it in an ironic way anymore. Be earnest and sincere and say, This is a great brand, goddamnit. An icon! People can't appreciate something unironically unless the thing itself is earnest as hell. So we leaned all the way in.

We even made special 750-mL champagne bottles that were released in limited supply in select cities. Suddenly people were racing around town, calling every liquor store, hoping they could find a $2 bottle of beer.

Why?

Because it was the *Champagne* of Beers, of course.

★

GUINNESS

I GOT A CALL from Guinness's head of global marketing one morning.

"Fly to London and have lunch with me."

Their classic Irish stout was still doing great. The problem, she would tell me, was that anytime they tried to innovate, it never seemed to capture the attention of craft beer drinkers and catch on beyond the initial launch.

She asked me to visit their St. James's Gate Brewery in Dublin and then come up with some ideas.

And that started this whole journey where I would take a quite different approach from all those previous heritage beer brands.

When I got to the brewery, I was flabbergasted because we didn't see any beer being made. They took us through the Guinness Storehouse, which is the number-one tourist attraction in Ireland, and all we saw was marketing, marketing, and more marketing. Old posters and ads hung everywhere, interactive exhibits on the brand, and even an atrium shaped like a pint of Guinness.

It was all very cool, but I kinda felt like I was in a Hard Rock Cafe.

Guinness is very proud of their marketing. And they should be. It's some of the best TV marketing of the twentieth century, especially Jonathan Glazer's artsy 1999 black-and-white commercial in which surfers ride waves among charging horses. Very cinematic. It always wins any poll or contest rating the best commercials of all time.

Being American, though, all I could think about was the craft beer revolution going on back home. So I told them, "You need to stop thinking like a marketer and start thinking like a brewer again."

I believed the key to innovation for Guinness was simply to be a brewer again. To move brewing to the forefront and remind people that Guinness actually makes beer, great handcrafted beer, and had started doing it a good two centuries before the term "craft" beer had ever been uttered.

They took me deep into the bowels of the brewery; they said the last non-employee who had been allowed to do this was Tom Cruise. It was like Willy Wonka's stout factory. It's automated, of course, as big, modern breweries have to be, and there's nothing wrong with that.

But St. James's Gate is set on a massive, multiacre facility. Why not take a tiny part of that and use it to make craft beers? As with Red Kamel, I thought they could make a hip, cool, startup brand within their overall brand. In a very organic way, it would build a pathway for Guinness to innovate beyond their supersuccessful, extremely iconic stout.

The easiest thing to do was to just open their pilot brewery to the public. This was where, for over one hundred years, they had made beers in smaller batches to test recipes. Why were they making beers no one ever got to taste? This wouldn't just be an innovation product, as many brands do; it would be an entire innovation platform. A craft brewery within Guinness. In November 2015, they literally lifted the doors of the pilot brewery to the public for the first time ever, fittingly calling it Open Gate Brewery.

The tagline was "Anything we can dream up, we get to brew up."

It was an immediate hit. People were stoked to see "what else" Guinness's top beer makers, whom we dubbed "The Brewers Project," could produce.

As with Camel, I began to dig through Guinness's archives and found all the old recipes. Before Arthur Guinness became the king of stout, he had made all kinds of styles.

I knew that if we brought some of these historical recipes back, it would help Guinness be seen as more than simply a big global brewery owned by Diageo and trying to fit into the growing craft beer movement. Instead, it would show that Guinness didn't need to fit into the craft beer scene because it had always been there, making a wide range of incredibly interesting beers for over 250 years.

(This strategy would be the exact opposite of that of Anheuser-Busch InBev, which around the same time tried to overcome similar fears of the growing craft beer movement by simply swooping in and acquiring already successful microbreweries such as Goose Island and many others.)

The brewers reinterpreted two-hundred-year-old porter recipes we'd found in Guinness recipe books deep in their archives. They brewed beers like the brand's first-ever commercial lager, Hop House 13, named after the original storehouse for hops at St. James's Gate. There wasn't even any huge Guinness branding on it. It was a smash, increasing Guinness's overall sales in Europe by 2 percent. That's a huge number for such a big brand.

In fact, this project was such a success that Guinness decided to do it again on a much larger scale in America. In 2019, an entire Open Gate Brewery was launched in Baltimore, the first Guinness brewery in the United States in sixty-four years. Since it opened, it has been incredibly well received, producing Guinness beers that are nothing like their long-famous stout: lagers, white ales, even IPAs.

We boosted their self-esteem so much that they now have plans to open a Guinness Chicago in time for St. Patrick's Day 2023. I sure hope to be there!

AUTHENTICITY IS EVERYTHING—
HOW DO YOU CREATE IT?

The Internet Will Reveal Any Lie Eventually

You MIGHT WORRY about how you can be authentic when you're inherently try-ing to get people to buy your brand.

My thinking is that you do that by *not* making the transactional nature of brands the most important part of them.

I've already told you how Gyro Worldwide was less an advertising agency than a performance art project. When that was most evident—say, with the G*Mart pop-up—I was constructing a sort of public double-blind taste test of the eye, trying to prove that, at its best, advertising is truly indistinguishable from art.

As trolls par excellence, we rebranded cans of SPAM as MEAT FLAPS, even putting them underneath spotlights as if they were literal works of art, selling them right next to rare PUMAs. Sometimes we even charged more for the SPAM, trying to show consumers how easily they were being fooled by slick packaging.

In 2008, after we sold Sailor Jerry to WGS, I felt that it was finally time to close Gyro Worldwide and put our childish pranks behind us. Or at least pretend we were doing so.

(Gyro Worldwide would be doing performance art even until its final days, when we released a fake book called *Virus: The Outrageous History of Gyro Worldwide*, written by a made-up French academic, Harriet Bernard-Levy, PhD, under the imprint of a phony publishing company whose address was actually a strip club in Regina, Saskatchewan. We sent signed copies of the book to all our Madison Avenue competitors with a handwritten note from me that said essentially, "I know my work has inspired and influenced you for years ..." A further troll implying that they had been aping our vibe, which they clearly had.)

Our truly final troll, however, was in the name change. There was an ad agency in London also called Gyro. They had just been bought by some VC firm and were going to expand all over the planet. Problem was, I owned the name Gyro in the United States. So the CEO of the other Gyro flew all the way to Philly to see if we could peacefully coexist and both use the same name.

"This is America," I told him. "And here, it's our duty to sue you."

I was kidding, playing hardball mostly as a joke to see how far I could take things. But he turned white as a ghost. Long story short, I left the meeting with an extra "undisclosed amount" in my pocket for a name that I was already planning on changing.

We reopened our agency under the name Quaker City Mercantile, determined to focus our efforts almost exclusively on booze and to also be a lot more grown-up.

We would now deliberately separate church from state, if you will. In other words, at Quaker City Mercantile, we would do brand work for other booze brands, such as our continuing relationship with Hendrick's. It would be a true money-making venture—how we make our BREAD.

Meanwhile, I had big plans to finally extend my creativity to brands that we would create, control, and, for the first time, fully own. That would be our BUTTER.

Instead of, say, Big Tobacco or German sporting goods companies funding our performance art, now *we* would, funded by our client work. (And we'd start using our best creative grenades to go viral with certain spirits releases.)

When we rebranded as Quaker City Mercantile, I hung original Shepard Fairey prints of Noam Chomsky and Joe Strummer in my new office. They are signed and quite special to me (not least because he misspelled "Proffessor" on the Chomsky one). But Shepard's work used to drive me crazy. Because I'd always wonder, What's the difference between him and me? Why is he an artist, and I'm not?

Is what I do "art"? I have always been reluctant to consider myself an artist.

I just have this insatiable desire to create and launch ideas into the world. In my early days, this urge was sated by crazy ideas and stunts such as Zipperhead, G*Mart, *Bikini Bandits*, and *Evil Empire*. I just had this urge to see what would happen. I guess I still do.

I literally say to myself, "Wouldn't it be funny if . . . ?" And then I go out and do it.

So is that art?

Yes, I think it is the very definition of art.

Art for art's sake.

But I could never take myself that seriously.

I think I'm self-aware enough to know that, like anyone else's, my shit stinks sometimes.

Similarly, I used to think I wanted to be a musician. I even had a band called Hair Club for Men. (We called it that because I had a shaved head.) Jon Wurster, who was our drummer, went on to play with Superchunk, the Mountain Goats, and Bob Mould. We were talented, but we didn't take ourselves that seriously.

I could never understand bands that took themselves so seriously. Dude, you're singing songs about dragons and trolls and girls! What you're doing is ridiculous.

And that doesn't mean it isn't awesome, but in your eyes, are you "authentic," are you making art, only if you *say* you're making art? If you make a whole big ordeal about what a great artist you are?

I wouldn't want that kind of pretense to surround my booze brands. We are craftspeople, sure, but not in that annoying hipster sense. We just quietly go about making great stuff. And I think our fans appreciate that. They know we have integrity.

I actually think it's because of that lack of pretense, because of not acting like we're great craftsmen, great artists, that our fans know we actually are authentic.

Look at Sailor Jerry. We were so careful with Norman Collins's legacy and image. The people who love his tattoos are very impassioned, and they wouldn't have put up with any BS. Of course, I've neglected to mention so far that Norman was a teetotaler, and now we were making a rum named after him.

How do you justify that?

You don't. You can't.

But you don't lie.

You don't create fake stories about how much Norman loved his spiced rum daiquiris.

"No, he didn't!" the fans would say.

And if we had said that kind of bullshit on the label, people would have immediately called us out on it.

Look at Templeton Rye. For years, they claimed that their mash bill was based on some old Al Capone recipe for bootlegged whiskey that they had discovered in an attic or some such thing. Wow, what a cool story! Unfortunately, from what I have read, it's just not true. They were sourcing the same 95 percent rye from MGP that everyone else was. And bloggers and people on social media had a field day ripping them to shreds, which is still reverberating today.

Their lie might have worked twenty years ago, when you could artistically cloak brands in an onion of lies, but that stuff doesn't work today. The spirits world has matured so much that you can't fool people anymore.

You have to be authentic, or you'll eventually be fucked.

The people you're selling to are just too smart.

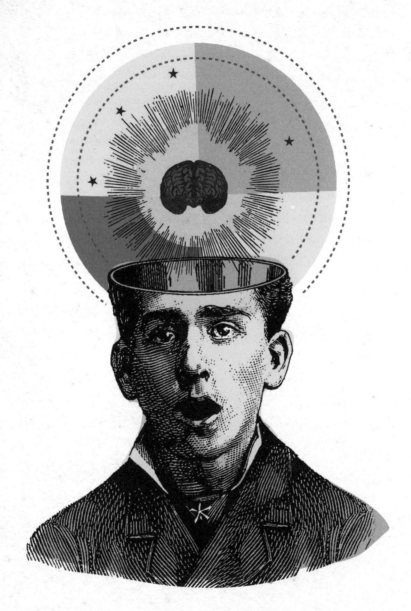

Fig. 32 There Are No Small Minds, Only Small People

LESSON 5
DON'T DUMB IT DOWN
Let the Mainstream Discover You

AND THAT'S WHY you should never dumb your brand down.

One of my employees once told me that we make things too complicated.

I said, "You need to make things that complicated to maintain people's interest! Successful brands have to work on multiple layers all at once. They need to be interesting enough that they capture your attention in the first place, but they also need to have enough depth that you keep coming back for more."

In other words, we need to layer these onions together for each and every brand.

Especially in this day and age, when everyone's head is tucked into their phone.

When you make something too simplistic, the consumer only needs to scratch the surface and then move on. That's the case with almost every movie and TV show these days. Certainly every Instagram, YouTube, and TikTok video.

A few minutes or even seconds in, you realize you can play a game on your phone or check your email while "watching" this streaming show and not miss a thing. There's nothing there.

(That's surely why that "Are you still watching?" pop-up happens on Netflix every so often. Even they know most of their shit is completely dispensable.)

It's likewise the case with all these spirits brands. They seem interesting, and then you flip the bottle, see "Distilled in Indiana," realize they're an upstart just sourcing their whiskey from MGP, and move on. There's nothing compelling to keep you interested.

(Maybe they too should have a pop-up: "Are you still drinking this crap?")

You can enchant people only through complexity.

The Simpsons is a great inspiration to me because it's a show that seemed so dumb at first but was actually very complex. And it became even richer with each season. That's why I think it has become such a cultural landmark.

Outsiders saw an immature cartoon about a dumbass dad and his hell-raising son, while the obsessives who watched and rewatched and quoted and referenced every episode knew how smart it actually is. It made the true fans feel as if they were in on a little secret.

Despite being the most famous cartoon of all time, despite being the longest-running scripted show of all time, *The Simpsons*' true greatness lies in how they've never actually pursued mainstream success. That sounds pretty funny for a show that has probably made Fox tens of billions of dollars, but if you think about it, *The Simpsons* got weirder as time went on, as they added more characters, more inside jokes, more callbacks. They literally forced their audience to grow with them.

You don't get the joke? Well, keep up, then, dummy!

Season one, they're doing simple gags about Homer working at a nuclear power plant and carelessly causing reactor meltdowns. By season four, they're doing truly dark episodes about Homer having a heart attack or Marge feeling disconnected from her husband, all the while offering obscure references to *The Music Man*; *Sophie's Choice*; Abraham Lincoln's mother, Nancy, who died of a rare milk sickness; and the experimental Godfrey Reggio documentary *Koyaanisqatsi* (did you catch that one?).

The show is still funny, obviously, if you don't get some *A Streetcar Named Desire* or *Clockwork Orange* callout. But if you do, it is much more gratifying and enjoyable. That's their brand mysticism.

I know I, like most people, would sometimes see a reference on *The Simpsons* and not get it until I stumbled upon the source material years later. And that's exactly what I like to do with my own brands.

I design them for:

The Cutting Edge of the Mainstream

In other words, not something so weird and hip that only a few hundred people could possibly understand it. Instead, something that is on the verge of cutting edge but able to emerge into a mainstream brand down the road. Like *The Simpsons*, I don't expect anyone to instantly digest what one of my brands is fully about the first time they encounter it—though they should certainly still be able to enjoy it on a surface level.

For instance, college kids—*legal-drinking-age adults*, of course—love Sailor Jerry because it's cheap and boozy and good for getting drunk on a budget. But maybe one day they'll be sitting around the dorm, staring at an empty bottle, and start wondering who Sailor Jerry was. Maybe they'll Google his name and start digging deeper, start realizing he was a real man with a fascinating biography, and learn how critical he was to tattoo culture. Soon they'll be reading about servicemen in the Pacific during World War II.

It's like a Wikipedia page where you keep clicking link after link after link until you're way down the rabbit hole.

Next time these college students are partying with a bottle of Sailor Jerry, you better believe they'll tell their other legal-drinking-age buddies, "Hey, did ya know that . . . ?"

Meanwhile, Captain Morgan starts looking like nothing more than a cartoon pirate who stands in a funny way.

Are you still watching?

Are you still drinking this crap?

IF YOU WENT TO A FANCY PANTS BUSINESS SCHOOL, I PROBABLY WON'T HIRE YOU

I'M HARDLY ONE to talk about higher education, as I wasn't exactly "college material." But maybe that's why, unlike most CEOs, I have very little interest in hiring people with MBAs from the country's top business schools. I'm not seduced by them whatsoever.

Wharton, the University of Pennsylvania's business school, often ranked the best in the nation, is just two miles away from our offices, a straight shot west on Walnut Street. So it's not surprising that fresh-faced Wharton MBAs often come over and try to tell me what I'm doing wrong and what they want to do for me and how I should start running my business and how much richer they could make both of us.

I admire the confidence, but I'm rarely impressed because they rarely have the kind of deeply weird ideas that I'm looking for.

I really feel like these "elite" schools crush creativity in people. The ability to come up with original ideas is deprogrammed from them. I see that every time I talk to an MBA. The schools teach them too many damn rules!

They teach them to be too smart.

I think business schools beat the sense of wonder and enchantment out of people.

My experience is that these people are often so concerned with getting good grades that they forget how to take chances. They do things too much by the rules because doing anything outside the lines might ruin their perfect GPAs and chance of adding "summa cum laude" to their résumés.

Ben Franklin didn't discover electricity because he read some case studies at Wharton. He discovered electricity because he was curious and went outside in the rain and flew a kite with a key on it.

This is yet another reason so many big booze brands lose their magic. They start finding a little success based on their founders' passion and intuition and then suddenly think they need CEOs and CFOs, and where do they turn? Business schools. Suddenly all the authenticity, all the weirdness in the brand is stripped away in favor of "monetizing" and ROI and other words from the MBA glossary.

No matter the industry, many of its major brands are completely run by MBAs from Harvard, Wharton, and the like. These people rarely have any passion for whatever they are currently selling; pull up the LinkedIn pages for many of them and you'll see that they bounce from the C-suite at Kellogg's to Crest and on to Cheetos—it doesn't really matter.

But I say it takes a special kind of STOOPID to do what I do successfully.

Fig. 33 The Ivy League Pipeline

To be truly creative, you need to be fearless. There's no textbook or business lecture that will tell you the key to success is spending years filling your brain with arcane and esoteric information . . . and then mashing it together in weird and wonderful ways that investors would never understand.

But you need to have this freedom!

That's the only way you will ever create fresh patterns, connections, and narratives. The fewer rules you follow, the fewer shackles you have holding you back from accomplishing something.

You can't be worried about what your professors back at B-School will say or what future business classes will think when they study you. If those people knew so much, they probably wouldn't be in business school.

They'd actually be running a successful business.

SO WHOM DO I HIRE?

CREATIVELY CURIOUS PEOPLE with little to no experience.

Zip, nada, zilch.

Because I want to train them. I want them to learn the way we learn things.

Or if they do have experience, maybe it's a *different* kind of experience. I'm looking for curious, culturally intelligent people with street smarts.

I rarely look at résumés when I'm conducting a job interview. Instead, I might ask the candidate, "What books do you read?"

Or I'll ask who their favorite poet is. Someone who spent the last two years in business school almost certainly won't even have an answer.

Or a favorite philosopher. Another question I love to ask.

What's the last band you went to see?

What movie is going to win Best Picture this year, and why?

My favorite job interview question: Tell me a joke.

I am trying to get the candidates to show me that they are curious. That they have lived a life of curiosity leading up to this meeting with me.

I want them to still have their imagination yet still be so dumb that they don't know any better about what the possibilities are in my world.

We also hire only local people, right out of school. I don't pay for anyone to relocate to Philadelphia.

As you can imagine, I'm an interesting person to work for. Maybe you think I sound like an asshole. And to some degree, it's true. People either end up working for me for thirty years . . . or they run screaming out the door a few hours into their first day in the office. I don't blame them.

I often joke that when I hire you, I'm indoctrinating you into my cult. But I think my passion and excitement are infectious. You're going to be paid well and ultimately do something you believe in.

I'm not sure you can say that if you take your MBA and go work for Kellogg's.

ART IN THE AGE

Pivot Quickly, Pivot Hard, Pivot Constantly

BY 2008, I WAS COCKY ENOUGH to think I could put anything in a bottle and sell billions of cases of it—because I'm a genius, right?

I would have a rude awakening with my first attempt to strike out on my own: something called Root.

By now you know I love history, I've always loved history, and I had been kicking around this idea for an alcoholic root beer spirit. The first commercial root beer, which was nonalcoholic, debuted at the Philadelphia Centennial Exposition in 1876. Delving deeper into its history, though, I realized that it had been spawned by Native Americans who had introduced root tea to settlers in the 1700s. And those teas had been very much alcoholic.

It was the temperance movement, in fact, that turned root beer nonalcoholic. I think they wanted to trick Pennsylvania coal miners into drinking it. That's why the term "beer" was tacked on. Same thing with ginger "ale." A temperance movement trick that just stuck, and no one really thinks about it anymore.

Root would be the first time I would ever have to actually produce the liquid myself. In the past, I had come up with the brand idea and done all the marketing, but WGS had homed in on the flavor profile and spent all their cash on development and then distribution. They were taking on all that risk. So Root would be a lot trickier than I expected.

My friend Reverend Michael Allen—an ordained minister, chef, and artist—and I created a liquid profile in miniature that was exactly what I wanted Root to taste like. I wanted it to use North American herbs (Pennsylvania is naturally replete with ingredients such as anise, birch bark, cloves, cardamom, and spearmint) and pure cane sugar, and I wanted it to be organic. We found a place in Los Angeles, Greenbar Distillery, that could scale up our recipe in commercial quantities.

When it was coming time to launch Root, I thought it would be smart to create an overall brand home for it to live under—something separate from QCM—even though I wasn't a distiller and didn't (yet) have a distillery. I had, of course, done the same thing for Sailor Jerry, which likewise didn't have a distillery but did have the Sailor Jerry store, a place that gave everyone some sense of where the rum brand originated from, a place for people to go to, a place for fans to pay homage.

I would do the exact same thing for Root, creating Art in the Age of Mechanical Reproduction, a DIY artists collective and store located on the same Old City block where the Sailor Jerry store was and G*Mart had once been. The name came from a 1936 essay by Walter Benjamin, *The Art in the Age of Mechanical Reproduction*. What that essay basically says is that the more art is reproduced, the more it loses its aura, and the more it loses its intrinsic value.

It's why you need to see art in person.

Our art, of course, would be the eventual unveiling of Root.

The store opened in 2008, about a year before Root would be released. We sold handmade products: custom wallpaper, stationery, housewares, artisan fragrances, private label T-shirts, even Mennonite quilts. This was before all that "maker" shit pervaded Etsy and the rest of the internet. Before Brooklyn became annoying. Before fucking Edison bulbs and reclaimed wood were signifiers of "cool urban cocktail bar."

Off-premise spirits sales were superimportant to us, more important than on-premise sales (in other words, bar sales), something that was heretical in the spirits business during that era. The problem was that in Philadelphia at the time, it was illegal for a distillery to sell spirits from their own location.

What we were allowed to do was offer free samples, however. Which we did when Root came out.

And people loved it!

It was a huge fucking hit.

The Art in the Age store became a sort of glorified, experiential, perpetual pop-up that allowed us to get tons of people to come taste our new product for free. And it totally worked!

It soon started to get buzz around the entire East Coast.

Since we were only selling it in Pennsylvania liquor stores, though, people started crossing the border from New York, New Jersey, Maryland, and Ohio to load up, reminding me of my PUMA drop days at G*Mart. I was soon getting requests from all over the country.

I began to see Art in the Age as housing a full lineup of root-based liqueurs, so we quickly introduced three more: Rhubarb, Sage, and Snap, a gingerbread-flavored spirit.

Unfortunately, because of this meteoric success, our costs were growing like crazy. We had to keep ordering more glass and more liquid and paying more shipping costs, more taxes, and more insurance . . . ahhhhh!

Since William Grant & Sons had done the manufacturing for Sailor Jerry, we had never experienced, or truly realized, how quickly these kinds of costs can escalate—$100,000 here, another $30,000 there. It just kept getting bigger and bigger every day, and I was panicking.

WGS saw what was going on and immediately made an offer to buy it from us. This was only six months after Root's launch! I think they were worried that someone else would swoop in and grab it. (Incidentally, they bought Hudson Whiskey on the same exact day. We now handle their brand work too.)

So I sold Art in the Age and made a nice, tidy sum . . .

. . . and then I watched Root completely languish.

Because I didn't fully control it anymore.

It was one of those cases where this big company just had no idea what to do with such a weird product. But it wasn't really their fault. I didn't actually know what to do with it either. It wasn't something you drank neat. It was certainly not something you'd belly up to the bar and drink all night. It was good for use in baking, but that would make for a really expensive Bundt cake.

So what exactly was the purpose of Art in the Age? Who exactly would be a regular customer and keep buying bottles?

This was still in the early 2010s, before high-end mixology had really taken off in places outside New York and San Francisco. Craft cocktails really weren't in

Philadelphia yet, and I'll be honest, I knew nothing about mixology at the time. That would have helped.

Back then, I didn't know that some products are considered base spirits and others are what is known as modifiers, the supporting players in a cocktail. That would have theoretically been a wonderful role for any of the Art in the Age products except for two more disadvantages inherent in them: They were too boozy (at 80 proof) and way too expensive.

WGS couldn't take over the actual distilling and production of Art in the Age to reduce costs either because they didn't have the capability to make it organically.

Eventually WGS's sales team started completely ignoring Art in the Age. It was too hard to sell, especially compared to the rest of their luxury portfolio, which included Balvenie, Glenfiddich, and Hendrick's. All of these were, of course, quite easy to sell to bars.

(In hindsight, I think we expanded with the variants too quickly. If I'd known more about mixology and amaro and where tastes were headed, I think we would have stuck solely with Root and pushed it as a sort of American fernet or Jägermeister: a boozy, potent, wildly spicy and flavorful shot. I think we may have been just a little ahead of our time. Root was Fireball before Fireball, and much better made, but it would never have had the virality due to the cost.)

I was getting pissed at how my baby was being handled, so eventually I just said to WGS, "Guys, let's quit fighting about Art in the Age, and how 'bout you just give it back to me?"

They did!

I think it's an incredible testament to the quality of the people at WGS and my long-standing relationship with them that they agreed to give the brand back to me. It certainly went a long way toward preserving our twenty-eight-year marriage. I remain grateful.

Then Greenbar informed me that they didn't want to make it anymore; they had moved on to bigger things. I thought, Maybe I should just find another contract distillery. Or could I try to make it myself somehow. We were finally starting to sell pretty well—Root had gotten up to twenty thousand cases per year, which isn't bad—but that would take up the entire capacity for a lot of boutique distilleries.

I had no choice but to pivot and reimagine Art in the Age. In 2017, we stopped making the original four variants (which, oddly, helped them sell even better as true fanatics quickly stocked up before they were discontinued). The next incarnation of Art in the Age products would be all about foraged ingredients and natural flavors and made by my own distillery, which was finally opened in New Hampshire.

We introduced a Sierra fig cordial, a black trumpet blueberry cordial, a tamarind cordial, and a turmeric cordial. Having learned that people didn't need much of something so potently flavorful, we downsized the packaging to 375 mL and lowered the proof. But then we also upped the price, selling them for $50 a bottle.

It was a nice little business for a while.

I'll stress *little*.

Then luck struck me again: Pennsylvania liquor laws changed, and suddenly distilleries were allowed on-premise sales so long as your alcohol was produced within the state.

So I signed a deal with my buddy Robert Cassell, who has a great spot in Philadelphia called New Liberty Distillery. He created Bluecoat Gin, which maybe you've heard of, and is a renowned whiskey maker as well. His distillery would receive totes—one-hundred-something-gallon storage containers—of Art in the Age and Tamworth Distilling liquid produced in New Hampshire and then bottle them in Philadelphia, thus rendering them "Pennsylvania-made."

We could now use his distilling license to get a satellite license for our Art in the Age shop. This would allow us to serve cocktails made with our spirits and to sell our own bottles (and New Liberty's) straight from the store, skipping the three-tier system—where producers, distributors, and retailers/bars must all be separately owned entities—and at full margins to boot. I am obsessed with margins and circumventing the distributor conundrum—they take 30 percent and often don't do a damn thing for you.

Art in the Age transformed my thinking about the value of a booze brand having a retail store for on-premise sales. I'd love to use this model and replicate it across the country: Find a local partner distiller and, in exchange for using their local license, open stores where we do the same things.

You might think Root belongs in the "failure" column of my bio since it no longer exists. But it's hardly a failure. A failure is something you give up on before making any money back—and I'll tell you about a couple soon enough.

Instead, Root taught me everything about how critical focus and timing are for any product. I was able to be a sellout with it . . . and then still get it back with all my intellectual property! Because of Root, I created Art in the Age, and because of that, I stumbled onto an ingenious way to sell my products straight to consumers. *Philly Mag* even named Art in the Age the best secret bar in the city a few years back.

Most importantly, though, through all the struggles and pivots over the years, we've added layers and layers of meaning and mysticism to the Art in the Age brand. Twelve years ago, I couldn't have envisioned an Art in the Age onion looking the way it does now, but that's not a bad thing.

Those layers that have formed *do* create a value and depth and authenticity that you simply can't conjure out of thin air. That you can't create simply by launching a new brand with a cool name.

LESSON 6

THE MORE THINGS ARE REPRODUCED, THE MORE THEY LOSE THEIR MYSTICAL POWER

WHEN I THINK ABOUT ART AND THE AGE'S MISSION, I can't help but also think of Starbucks.

In 1992 or thereabouts, Howard Schultz invited me to Seattle to talk to him about what we might do for his then fledgling coffee company, which was in the process of developing a partnership with PepsiCo. He had seen our MTV spots and wanted to attach that same cool vibe to Starbucks.

I liked the guy immediately. At the time, Philadelphia didn't yet have a Starbucks location. And when Schultz—a tough Brooklynite from Canarsie—learned where I was from, he quickly filled me in on why that was.

"I hate Philadelphia!" he told me. I had to admire the honesty. "It'll be the last city I ever go to."

But he must have liked rapid expansion more than he hated Philly. A Starbucks was opened in Center City by 1995. Today there are over thirty thousand locations in the world.

We never ended up working with Schultz, but not because Starbucks wasn't cool. It was back then. It felt authentic too. Even by 1995, there simply weren't many places in America that offered made-to-order espresso and cappuccinos. It felt very European, very urbane. But today, of course, Starbucks feels like a McDonald's.

It's essentially what Walter Benjamin was saying: The more you create mass shit that is sold by places like Walmart and Amazon, or appears on every street corner, the more it loses its aura. People buy fleeting items at those places—light-bulbs and garbage bags and romance novels and fast-fashion T-shirts.

Not beautiful stuff they truly care about and will cherish for years.

Mass production also makes us lose what makes us special as human beings—we simply become mindless consumers. How can a cup of coffee be special if everyone on planet Earth can get the same green cup at any strip mall? If you run into a friend on the street, they aren't going to ask you about your cup of Starbucks—what would there be to tell them? That you needed a quick dose of whipped cream-covered caffeine, and it was highly accessible?

There's nothing there to enchant them.

Starbucks literally invented modern craft coffee culture in America, but the more they reproduced themselves, the more they lost any sense of their mission and the mystical power they once held over the nation's coffee drinkers.

You see this happen a lot with brands that were once small and hot. Being small and hot inherently brings in capital and demand, buzz and hype, MBAs and CEOs, expansion and ultimately overexpansion, and then scrutiny.

I worry about that a bit with my biggest successes—Hendrick's is hardly some niche gin these days; it sells well over a million cases per year. But I feel that if we continue our storytelling, if we continue to lean into the mysticism we built these brands on, if we never betray our mission, then the potential lack of authenticity that comes with growth can be overcome. It's not easy, but it's doable.

Starbucks, in my opinion, didn't romanticize their own lore enough. Why did they quit talking about what their name means? (It's a character from *Moby Dick*;

did you even know that?) Why don't they lean more into that once iconic twin-tailed mermaid logo? (It was meant to evoke the seafaring history of coffee and Seattle's location as a seaport by showing this seductive siren of Norse mythology—that's cool! But have you ever heard them promote that?)

Instead, they expanded on pure B-school rationality: We make better coffee than a pot of drip Folger's from the gas station, and we'll give you a "third place" to sit all day if you feel like trying to get some work done while tourists chatter around you.

But once every neighborhood started getting hipster coffee shops with better coffee; once every place started talking about Ethiopia and Sumatra, how they source their beans, how they make latte art; once every roastery offered a clean, cozy place to chill out with your laptop, Starbucks was toast. They no longer felt authentic. It was still reasonably good coffee, but you were only excited if it was 6 a.m. and you stumbled upon it in an airport terminal.

That's why I think it's silly when spirits brands talk only about their liquid. It's too rational. Someone can always make better, older, and even cheaper liquid than you!

Guinness does a great job of being an old, massive brand that still maintains authenticity. I think that's because they lean into being the embodiment of the Irish people. Irish pubs are all over the world, from Alabama to Zaire, and all of them serve Guinness.

They rarely talk about their liquid, and when they do, it's more to say, Hey, we don't sell stout. *We sell Guinness.* In that way, they literally don't even allow themselves to have a competitor. They even have that unique ritual of their 119-second pour—I imagine it's not truly necessary for taste, but it feels so romantic. They actually make you wait to drink their beer!

Looking at Guinness, I knew when it came time to finally start my own distillery, it had to be completely built on this type of enchantment and lore and, most importantly, onion-wrapped layers of storytelling.

And it would all have to start with the distillery's location.

TAMWORTH DISTILLING AND MY COLONEL KURTZ MOMENT

When It All Came Together

MANY MODERN CRAFT DISTILLERIES tend to be in industrial parks and suburban parking lots on the far edge of town. They're not a destination, they're not romantic, and they certainly aren't enchanting.

I don't know if you've ever been to Lynchburg, Tennessee, where Jack Daniel's is located, but it's magical. There's nothing there! You drive for an hour and a half south of Nashville, on country roads without stoplights, and then all of a sudden, you're at this oasis of whiskey.

I liked that feeling and was intrigued by the idea of a distillery itself having a sense of place. I wanted to one-up Jack Daniel's, even, and build a distillery in the most idyllic, most remote place in the country. I had the perfect spot too.

My mother's ancestors had been among the original colonists who came to New Hampshire in 1631, just a few years after the colony was founded. New Hampshire was very different from the Massachusetts Bay Colony because it was founded by merchants, not Puritans, which could be where the state's "Live Free or Die" mindset comes from.

My ancestors eventually settled in a town called Meredith on the western shore of Lake Winnipesaukee. I spent every summer there as a kid. My uncle, Big Buck Bucklin, was the town fire chief and a local legend who inspired the Moose character in the *Archie* comics. (True story—he was best buddies with Bob Montana, who created them.)

I loved it up there.

So with my share of our profits from the Sailor Jerry sale, I decided to buy some land and give my kids the same experience that I'd once had. I began looking thirty minutes north of Meredith at the foot of the White Mountains. The real estate agent tried to talk me out of it. She said that people like me usually buy in Vermont. That is where all the rich New Yorkers buy.

"AND THAT IS EXACTLY WHY WE ARE NOT BUYING IN VERMONT!" I told her.

Why does everyone always want you to do the same thing that everyone else is doing? How can you get inspired by that? The last place I want to be is where a bunch of entitled, snooty people from New York City are.

I prefer the hardscrabble White Mountains, home to my forebears. I knew that was a location that would cultivate my curiosity.

For instance, when researching the area where I thought I wanted to live, I was intrigued to discover that in 1830, something called the Siege of Wolves had happened in the town of Tamworth on a spot called Marston Hill. Six hundred men, commandeered by a General Quimby of Sandwich, engaged against a "large number" of wolves that had been killing the local sheep and calves at night. Afterward, the dead wolves were brought to town for a celebratory feast where everyone finished off an entire barrel of rum. This was all, remarkably, reported in the *New York Times*.

You can't make up that kind of mysticism about a place.

There's more: Henry David Thoreau visited Tamworth in 1858 and wrote about it in his journal. From what I've been told, this is why a lot of scholars and professors had summer cottages here.

Eventually the real estate agent took us five miles up the hill—which is actually more like a mountain—and showed us a house called Great Hill Farm. It was built in the 1740s but totally redone in 1913. The architect also designed Teddy Roosevelt's summer retreat on Campobello Island in the Canadian province of New Brunswick.

This was also what had originally been known as Marston Hill—the very hill where the siege had happened.

As a history lover, I was immediately enchanted.

Then I learned that one of our neighbors would be George Cleveland, President Grover Cleveland's grandson—it's one of those weird, unbelievable-seeming

American facts that he is still alive. He told me that Tamworth was located on what's known as a ley line, just like Sedona, Stonehenge, and the Great Pyramids at Giza. Ancient people, and even some today, believe these lines create a weird energy that you can tap into. He said that was why I was so drawn to the town.

I don't know if that's true, but I wanted to believe.

All this enchantment, all this mysticism, all this history and lore seemed to be centered around Tamworth. The world seemed to be conspiring in my favor.

So I bought the farm.

Then I bought the local Village Store, which had stood on literal Main Street since 1826. Then I bought an inn, and suddenly I felt like Colonel Kurtz, building my crazy little utopia and attracting a following of like-minded tribesmen and -women.

(I currently own four of the ten buildings in the entire town. The ones I don't own include a country doctor farm museum; America's oldest summer stock theater, The Barnstormers [started by President Cleveland's youngest son, Francis]; and a general store called the Other Store.)

When it came time to build Tamworth Distilling in 2015, my goal was to literally go where no other distillery had gone before, to explore everything that is possible as you transmute the life force of plants and grains into spirits.

If Art in the Age was inspired by Walter Benjamin's essay, I decided to take Tamworth Distilling a step further. All the brands we would create would bring the storytelling and mythos of the area to life. Many would be based on all the great New England transcendentalists from the region—Ralph Waldo Emerson, Henry David Thoreau, Frederic Henry Hedge, Alexander von Humboldt, and the like. They had all raised the alarm at the dawn of the industrial age, and with this company, I didn't want to lose sight of that.

(We're legally registered as Transcendental Spirits, actually, but we go by Tamworth Distilling.)

I began to think of Tamworth Distilling in two ways:

1. *As a classic, wilderness-to-bottle distillery where we could grow grain and forage local ingredients for our gins and other spirits.*

2. *And as a sort of test kitchen for our big-money client work with Quaker City Mercantile.*

At the start of the book, I told you I knew literally nothing about gin when I created Hendrick's Gin. Now I know everything about everything because my Tamworth team distills it.

I think one reason the advertising industry is collapsing is that agencies are generalists. They don't really know anything about the products they're working on beyond the surface level. All they know is how to make wacky ads.

My goal with Tamworth was to learn more about the spirits industry than even our clients knew so I could be the definitive authority when they came to me. If I was an authority, I could make the definitive case to hire us.

If a big cognac producer came to me, I wanted to be able to say, Here's all we know about making brandy or whiskey or gin or amaro. Here's all our research has shown; here are all the ingredients we've explored; here are all the formulas we've tried. Even past that point: Here are all the glasses we've bottled in, all the bottle shapes we've worked with, molds we've made, and so on.

My feeling is that creativity is spiritual. It's a religion. Creating is a form of worship. It gives context and meaning to our chaotic existence. I say, Stop mindlessly consuming and make something. Otherwise, what the fuck are you on the planet for?

And actually, there's a third way I think of Tamworth Distilling now:

1. *As an utterly pure performance art project of a whole different kind than Gyro in its early days.*

With Tamworth, I can proudly say that I don't create things to fill a marketing niche, I create things that *I* would actually buy.

And I assume there are other people out there just like me. So if I make things I find interesting, that maintain my interest, chances are other like-minded people out there will agree. They will appreciate the depth and passion behind each thing we put in a bottle.

That's likewise why I don't think we have much problem attracting talented people to come work for us, even if we are in the middle of nowhere. Because they are actually allowed to think and create and do one-of-a-kind projects. We're not just creating brands; we're creating products that have integrity, that they're proud to have a part in creating.

In comparison, if they got a job at a major distillery, they might be just pushing buttons that make vodka.

Oh, my god, I'd be bored out of my skull!

In some ways, Tamworth is easier than anything I've ever done before. With global brands such as Hendrick's, we might need to figure out a way to create a new variant that sells one million cases per year. At Tamworth, I might need to sell only fifty bottles of some weird new gin made out of basil and local cantaloupe.

I can afford to be creative, risky, strange, and I guess, to some delicate flowers, even offensive!

I can also afford to be that way because we are financially very conservative: We don't borrow money, and we don't have VC funding us. My Pennsylvania Dutch frugality runs deep.

Mind you, I have no interest in selling out ever again. I have no interest in Tamworth Distilling being acquired by Beverage Megacorp International. I don't aspire to be that dude who does all the celebrity tequilas with Turtle from *Entourage*. If I did, I would have gone about things a whole different way.

My raison d'être these days is to see how far we can go, to see what the boundaries of distilling are, to explore the vast frontier of any project's conceptual and philosophical intent.

If we make money along the way, great.

If we just have a blast, that's fine too.

But over my many years, this attitude has often led to me making money—sometimes a lot of money. (Again, see Gyro's stunts.)

So far, in just about six years, we've created an extraordinary range of products, not just the same vodka/gin/bourbon that every craft distillery seems to make. We've got apple jack, VSOP brandy, pommeau, aquavit, winter wheat whiskey, rye whiskey, straight corn whiskey, and dozens of gin varietals.

We don't have this many stock keeping units (SKUs) so that we can dominate shelf space; we have this many because we think we can do them better and more interestingly than anybody else.

We've produced truly one-of-a-kind, what-the-fuck tamarind and turmeric cordials, a black trumpet mushroom wild blueberry cordial, something called Black Jupiter modeled after the French aperitif *vin de noix*, and a cherry liqueur based on an old Martha Washington recipe.

We've created what is essentially a little Disney World, but for spirits. People drive to Tamworth from all across the country. And if someone has made this long drive, there needs to be something fun to do once they arrive. They aren't just buying a bottle of bourbon and driving back home.

Even more importantly, these people need to hear about us in the first place. Since the distillery is in the middle of nowhere, you're not going to accidentally just stumble upon it.

The one bad thing about Tamworth is, unlike Hendrick's or Sailor Jerry, we don't have the money or resources to constantly blast people with "awareness" campaigns.

That's where our creative grenades come in.

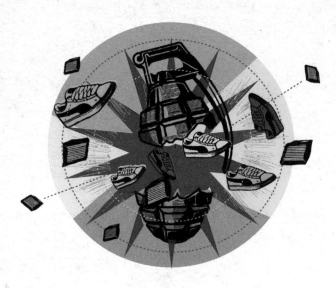

LESSON 7

LAUNCH CREATIVE GRENADES

Beaver Anus Whiskey and Drinking Dead People

IF PUMA HAD INTRODUCED ME to the concept of creative grenades through their limited shoe drops, with Gyro Worldwide, I was still using the idea mainly to troll the culture. Things like Derrie-Air and *The Evil Empire* were fun and got us loads of attention—and sometimes even made money!—but they weren't necessarily part of a larger purpose and certainly didn't help us build a cult of followers.

With Tamworth Distilling, however, I am finally able to use creative grenades as a layer of the onion, as part of our enchantment and mysticism, as a critical part of our marketing strategy—and I've gone more viral than ever.

I probably don't need to tell you that in many ways, it's harder to break through today. You have these incredible viral tools at your disposal, yet there are just so many websites, so much social media, so much content out there for people to consume that it can get lost in the shuffle. Something trends on Twitter in the morning and is forgotten by the afternoon. Someone likes a funny meme on Instagram and then quickly flips to the next photo.

The thing is, though, if something *truly* breaks through today, it spreads much faster and much more deeply than it did when I started out in the business.

Creative grenades are especially critical on a lean budget and when you're not a big dog. When I started out with PUMA, they didn't have much money, nor did they have great distribution channels; thus, we used limited-edition, buzzy products to get people talking.

Today, I face the same issues at Tamworth Distilling. We're a small, rural New Hampshire brand that is mostly sold only within the state. How am I going to get people in New York, San Francisco, London, and Tokyo to know we even exist?

Well . . . I suppose I could release a whiskey made from beaver anus.

One day I asked my distillery team, "With thousands of new distilleries already operating in America, what is the most differentiated liquid we could possibly make to set ourselves apart?"

"What do you got that is different from what everybody else is doing?"

They brought up the idea of castoreum.

Okay, it's not really beaver anus but rather a yellowish exudate that comes from the castor sacs, near the anal glands, of beavers. ("Beaver anus" is obviously much better for clickbait headlines.)

Castoreum wasn't on the Generally Recognized as Safe (GRAS) list—the FDA's list of legal additives—but that was good. It would mean no one else could legally use it before I got it approved. Which I did because I was able to prove to the FDA that castoreum had a historical precedent as a tincture, having been used as a food additive since the early 1900s.

Of course, this was not just a goofy ingredient to get internet clicks. New Hampshire has a big beaver population—a big beaver *problem*—and that would help inform our storytelling, help build the onion.

We took some of our two-year-old bourbon and added oil extract from the castor gland. It gave it this great flavor of leather and raspberry, which we bolstered with birch oil and Canadian snakeroot, a gingery wood spice. It tasted great and truly one of a kind, and it would also offer fun shock value when people found out what was in it.

We called it Eau de Musc (Water of Musk) and put a beaver on the label, bottling it under a classy new high-end line, House of Tamworth, which we sold for $65 per 200 mL bottle.

We got insane press. Maybe the best of my career up to that point. The *New York Post*, *Esquire*, *Thrillist*. All the local and national news channels. Threads on Reddit, massive shares on Twitter and Facebook. International coverage across the globe.

Getting a newspaper mention in Russian, written in Cyrillic, might not seem that valuable for a small New Hampshire brand. But it actually is. It makes a New Hampshire local feel special that he can get something the biggest oil oligarch in Moscow can't. But it also makes the Russian drinker mentally take note: Next time I'm in the States, I need to visit this crazy Tamworth place!

I knew we were onto something with Eau de Musc and wanted to try to repeat the success a year later.

In 2019, we produced our next House of Tamworth release, Graverobber. It was a maple-flavored whiskey made with, as we claimed on the label, "the spirits of the dead." (Our property had a malignant old maple tree whose roots just happened to burrow deep into a nearby Colonial-era cemetery.) This "evil yet divine" whiskey made of "sinister sap" didn't actually get much press that first year, but we sold a ton of it in 2020. (That's the thing about creative grenades. Sometimes they take a while to explode.)

I started thinking about how game and wildlife, foraging and nature seemed to be capturing people's imagination. And today's press is always looking for new stories to cover.

In 2020, we released The Deer Slayer, a venison-flavored whiskey. I had been inspired by reading about James Fenimore Cooper, whose last novel in his Leatherstocking Tales was called *The Deerslayer*. I loved that name and immediately registered it with the Department of the Treasury's Alcohol and Tobacco Tax and Trade Bureau (TTB).

I then challenged the distilling team to come up with something befitting the name. They took red deer venison from a local farm, hand-chopped the meat, and tossed it with cranberries, porcini mushrooms, juniper berries, and green peppercorns, then fermented it overnight to accentuate the gaminess before slow-smoking it over a mix of seasoned branches from New Hampshire's boreal forests. We then added that to a white wheat whiskey.

I think that got even more press than Eau de Musc!

The great thing is that each of these creative grenades was generating press and excitement from new factions and new outlets, not just, say, *Whisky Advocate*. The Deer Slayer, for instance, really started going viral on country music radio stations, of all places. Well, of course it would, we realized in retrospect. A lot of country music fans are both whiskey drinkers and big deer hunters.

Not all creative grenades work, though. You can't just think of some crazy, unfathomable, shocking bullshit and expect buzz every time.

Last year, we also released a House of Tamworth bottling called Corpse Flower, a brandy modeled off titan arum, whose petals smell of rotting meat. I challenged my distilling team to create a spirit that would smell awful while simultaneously tasting divine. A real mindfuck, hopefully. Using that same stinky durian fruit I recalled from my time in Chanthaburi three decades ago, plus indole fruit, and naturally isolating their most offensive molecules, they accomplished that task.

I'll be honest: It didn't get the press we had come to expect for House of Tamworth. Although it did get some, such as a piece by *Robb Report* pretty much wondering why anyone would want to drink something that smelled like death.

In retrospect, we were probably too clever there and maybe a little too cocky with our viral abilities.

Even so, I find that some journalists are very lazy these days. Oftentimes they'll literally just repeat whatever you give them in a press release, and if just one publication picks up the story, everybody else will roll with it as fact. They have to lest some other website get all the clicks.

I mentioned earlier that it became much harder to launch creative grenades once PUMA started becoming too big and making too much money. That's the case with most brands, but it hasn't been the case with Hendrick's. Maybe because, unlike with Tamworth, the creative grenades are often not related to the liquid. Don't get me wrong; we work closely with Hendrick's on each new variant, and they are all unique, differentiated, and delicious, but these releases often merely add new dimensions to our overall brand universe.

For Hendrick's creative grenades, we consider other avenues.

In early 2020, during the most unbearable doldrums of the COVID-19 pandemic, as everyone was stuck at home, exercising on their yuppie Pelotons, we launched the Hendrick's High Wheel. It was a full-blown intricate, old-timey penny-farthing bicycle with a forty-eight-inch-high front wheel, set up as a stationary bike atop some artificial grass adorned with rose petals, a nod to Hendrick's flavor profile.

It was meant to be a hilarious prank with a hilariously high price tag to match, but nevertheless, we sold eight of them instantly!

And the press quickly started covering it. Again, though, it wasn't the usual press that covers Hendrick's. We got stories in *Bicycling* magazine and *Travel & Leisure*. And the print edition of the *Wall Street Journal*. The visuals were just so shareable, good for a quick laugh online.

We had done something similar in 2016, when we made a Hendrick's-branded organ that had cucumbers for keys. We installed what we called the world's first-ever "Corgan" at the Toronto Eaton Centre and hired some of the city's top organists to play it while we offered gin-and-tonic samples to the crowd.

Despite how fun these stunts are, and how effective at getting the Hendrick's name out there, the ultimate goal of a creative grenade is to make sales. I think many of the most successful viral marketers forget this at times. Viral press is great, but if it doesn't lead to people buying your product, what's the point? You can't meet payroll each month with Instagram likes.

(This was an occasional failing on our part with our G*Mart trolls. Some of our products got a lot of people talking about how offensive or outlandish they were, but few people wanted to buy them.)

That's why we hope these House of Tamworth creative grenades, which are always superexclusive and superexpensive, will bring people toward our more mainstream, more affordable gins and whiskeys. Indeed, they have: Our sales were up 99.5 percent during the rolling two years of the pandemic, when creative grenades were our best way to market to people stuck at home.

Yes, these are ultimately publicity stunts, and publicity stunts have been going on forever. But what I particularly like about Tamworth's creative grenades is that they actually taste good (if not always smell good), further our brand mythology, and offer a shorthand for what we're ultimately about.

Eau de Musc and Graverobber and The Deer Slayer and, yes, even Corpse Flower are authentic expressions of our distillery's mission. They're not just publicity stunts dreamed up out of thin air.

They have a basis in the storytelling of Tamworth, in the organic ingredients we aspire to use, and in the localness of New Hampshire. And I love that.

USE RESTRICTIONS TO YOUR ADVANTAGE

As I just mentioned, the FDA has something called the GRAS list, ingredients that are "Generally Recognized as Safe."

What's interesting about spirits compared to other categories, even beer, is that there are very few spirit ingredients on the GRAS list. Thus, it would seem, our crazy experimentation is restricted by the government.

But, my name being Grasse, I thought we could start using the GRAS list restrictions to our advantage in the future.

I've hired full-time historians at Quaker City Mercantile, and one of their jobs is to find historical evidence of the use of weird ingredients in food, such as castoreum. Find that historical link, and the FDA and TTB will almost always accept the use of it in a spirit. And, as I mentioned regarding Eau de Musc, if you discover the ingredient and get it approved, you're naturally going to be the only spirits company actually using it in your products for quite a while. That's a huge advantage when it comes to having a differentiated liquid and garnering attention.

Likewise, it's no coincidence that we have built our distillery and our retail operations in restrictive "control states," where the government controls and sells all the liquor. Besides Pennsylvania and New Hampshire, there are fifteen others.

It seems counterintuitive to want the government to control our product sales, but I thought I could take advantage of the restrictions of a control state and reap the benefits. Mainly, instead of there being hundreds, if not thousands, of liquor store owners throughout New Hampshire and Pennsylvania, there's only one: the state itself. (That restriction actually makes Pennsylvania and New Hampshire the second- and third-largest single buyers of spirits in all of North America.)

So if I could convince New Hampshire's and Pennsylvania's one buyer to bring in all my products, then I knew I'd be stocked in every store in the state. And since they have a state mandate to "buy local," I'm already a step ahead of the big brands.

It's worked so far!

As have the "restrictive" liquor laws that allow me to own five liquor stores with full cocktail-bar components in Pennsylvania. It's really quite amazing and why I often call the state the land of milk and honey.

Don't complain about restrictions—those are just a fact of life—but instead ask yourself how they can force you to be even more creative with your work.

Fig. 34 The Original Stock Market

THE WORST BRAND I EVER CREATED

Spodee, Wine in a Milk Bottle

THEN THERE ARE SOME CREATIVE GRENADES that explode in your face.

The worst thing I ever launched was something called Spodee.

It was 2012, and QCM was doing really well, getting a lot of buzz, and taking tons of meetings. We had some people with a lot of money ask us to come up with something new and cutting edge for them.

Unfortunately, when there are lots of different partners involved, things can turn into a real shit show, and in this case, I broke two of my cardinal rules.

At the time we had restrictions on creating spirit brands with anyone besides William Grant & Sons. So we decided to come up with a wine product instead. Conveniently, I had been listening to a lot of blues music at the time and had just heard a great song from the 1940s: Stick McGhee's "Drinkin' Wine, Spo-Dee-O-Dee."

Oh, this is great! I thought.

I did a little research, and it turned out that wine "spodiodi" was a real thing made down South during the Depression. Essentially, destitute people would take cheap wine, mix it with moonshine, and add whatever other spices and ingredients they had around to make it palatable.

Unfortunately, the way this particular partnership was set up meant we weren't in charge of liquid development. Our partner was. And after nearly one hundred rounds of back-and-forth and our team complaining that the liquid was not up to our standards, we finally relented and said, "OK, let's roll with it."

Big, big mistake.

Spodee would combine port wine with chocolate sauce.

What the fuck were they thinking?

What the fuck were *we* thinking?

I didn't stick to my number-one rule: high-quality, differentiated liquid! And this liquid totally sucked. (If something isn't working, it's far easier to pivot the marketing in the future than to change the liquid, remember.)

We packaged it in an old-school milk bottle, the glass kind they used to drop off on your back porch in the 1950s. It was unique and looked cool, but we couldn't get the closure right. When the bottles shipped, they leaked all over the place.

It was a fucking train wreck.

And it would only get worse for us when we doubled down with Spodee White—basically a pineapple-tasting white wine port at 24 percent ABV. Almost like a pineapple vermouth.

It flopped even harder.

Yet, despite all these issues, I think we could have made this all work with a few tweaks. Because we did get the brand world right: the overall mysticism of this Depression-era-like product. In fact, you can still visit www.spodeewine.com and see our design work and some of our other ideas. I think they're pretty great even now.

If we'd had full control of the product, we could have quickly pivoted. Improved the closures, of course, and the purpose of Spodee. We should have positioned it as more of an offbeat fortified wine or something—Boone's Farm or Night Train for the broke millennial. That might have worked.

Or, if we had not put Spodee White in the damn milk bottle, we could have pitched it as a kind of tiki vermouth for mixologists. And we would probably have hit right as the tiki boom was coming.

Unfortunately, when there are partners involved, it's hard to quickly pivot and make the tweaks needed to make something work.

I think you can literally fix anything if you keep tinkering.

But with Spodee, we'll never know.

For now, it remains a massive failure I'll never forget.

FULL CONTROL

THERE'S THAT CLASSIC LINE; maybe it's Gilbert K. Chesterton. Whoever said it first, I was repeating it to myself all the time after the Spodee debacle: "I've searched all the parks in all the cities and found no statues of committees."

In retrospect, I realized that anytime we've had a problem launching brands, as with Spodee, it was because we weren't granted full control over the entire process. That sounds a bit arrogant, but it's true.

And *that*, I now realize, as we near the end of this book, is truly the secret ingredient.

Everything needs to be working together in concert for a brand to fully succeed, and that can happen only when the brand has a single overall auteur.

For instance, we once collaborated with one of Europe's largest distributors of spirits to create something called Prizefight, an Irish whiskey.

Everything was seemingly in place. The liquid was delicious, classic Irish whiskey, but finished in American rye casks. The concept was that this "transatlantic" brand would honor those Irish immigrants who came to America with nothing and then fought for everything.

The packaging was perfect, with the label looking like an old-time boxing poster for a long-forgotten bare-knuckle fight between Yankee Sullivan and John Morrissey, both Irish Americans.

We had the brand mysticism too. We'd built a massive onion of a brand that would reveal many intriguing layers (the California Gold Rush! Tammany Hall politics! Bill the Butcher!) the more you looked into it.

The problem was, our partners were laser-focused on getting Prizefight into Dublin's fanciest, most high-end cocktail bars. On winning over the coolest mixologists in Ireland. I thought this was absolutely the wrong strategy. We knew that in order to keep the brand financially viable, we had to also be focused on getting it moving in off-premise sales.

"You gotta stack this high at every freakin' retailer!" I told them. I implored them to pursue that avenue.

Don't get me wrong: High-end mixologists are great, but they are never going to buy enough bottles to keep your brand from going under. There just aren't enough of them.

Believe me, it takes a lot to make even a great brand stick. At QCM, we are adamant about being in a market only if we have "feet on the street." In other words, people to continually support the brand who can maintain traction after the initial launch event. You really need to work a market to make a brand stick.

That's why I believe what we should have done was try to blow up in Dublin, make the brand the biggest thing there, then move on to the rest of Ireland, and then, and only then, expand to other markets. Our partners could easily have used their retail heft and influence to get prominent shelf space and floor displays at every liquor store in Ireland, bolstered even further by in-person tastings that their team could have conducted nightly.

Instead, they threw fancy parties for snooty mixologists and took business-class flights to New York and Boston to try to launch the product further in the United States. Eventually they blew through all their cash much faster than they should have.

The people who tried Prizefight loved it. We had all the magical ingredients in place. It was just that very few people even knew it existed.

By the time there was a need for a second run on bottles, I saw that we were at the point of no return, and this brand was not going to succeed.

I refused to invest any more money, and I promised myself that it would be the last time I wouldn't have full control over a brand from creation to getting it into customers' hands.

SPIRITS AWARDS ARE WORTHLESS TOO

THE REASON I don't enter design awards competitions is the same reason I don't send out Tamworth Distilling products to be reviewed for any spirits awards. I feel that the last thing I want is for my competitors to be sitting around a table drinking Eau de Musc and comparing it to other, more traditional stuff.

Who cares whether the so-called standard-bearers think it's good or bad?

We're already going out of our way to do things differently. We didn't design our Chocorua Rye to be just another rye; we wanted it to be its own thing and for you to discover what makes it so special.

We don't want you to discover it because it has a stupid San Francisco Spirits Award gold medalist sticker on the bottle. No one purchases a bottle because of a stupid awards sticker!

(Did you know that in a lot of these contests, everyone pretty much just pays $550 per entry and then "wins" that award? Sounds like a scam to me.)

We want you to discover Chocorua Rye by stumbling upon this curious squared-off bottle in the store, with a label that doesn't look like a whiskey label but instead resembles an antiquarian book. It features in small print the entire text of Rh. S. S. Andros's haunting poem "Chocorua."

We want you to pick up this weird bottle, so different from every other, and learn that its mash bill is 100 percent a single crop of organic rye grain from Maine, house milled and distilled in the sour-mash style with local herbs and botanicals from our garden and the nearby woods.

Very few companies release a 100 percent rye whiskey these days. I doubt anyone else has ever printed an entire poem on their whiskey bottle. And some snotty critic is going to sit down in a hotel ballroom in a pretend lab coat, sniffing and drinking and comparing it to some rye whiskey sourced from MGP?

No, thank you.

The greatest award our products can win is turning strangers into lifelong fans. And you don't need to pay a $550 entry fee to attempt that.

I WANT TO BE THE HERMÈS OF BOOZE

AS WE NEAR THE END OF THIS BOOK, we can't ignore the fact that monumental, sweeping change is happening in all industries these days, and especially the alcohol industry.

As I write this, Uber has just acquired Drizly, the alcohol delivery service, for $1.1 billion. The COVID-19 pandemic only accelerated the changes that were already happening to how people buy booze (and everything else), as laws have gotten laxer and the major players have really begun to dominate.

What will happen when Amazon eventually figures out how to work around that three-tier system I mentioned earlier? What will happen when Amazon starts producing their own booze and is able to sell it for rock-bottom prices, shipped the same day and free via Prime?

I'll tell you what will happen: Most tiny alcohol brands will be completely fucked.

But I'm guessing Macallan won't. Dom Pérignon won't. Louis XIII won't.

Residing in the super high end of the market is the only protection from this kind of turbulence. It's the only way to be Bezos-proof. And furthermore, I believe, the more arcane the craftsmanship that goes into making something, the deeper the brand mysticism, the more intricate your onion, the more likely it will be to stick around through such upheaval. Ingredients will be more important than ever, and so will storytelling.

Every other part of a liquor brand—but especially the liquid—will be easily commoditized. Most people won't care because their Amazon bourbon will be $12 a bottle. You've already had a hint of this with all these upstart whiskey brands simply sourcing bourbon and rye from MGP in Indiana, and with Costco selling their Kirkland Signature house-branded spirits at rock-bottom prices.

That's why, to me, Hermès is so amazing, and what I aspire to with Tamworth.

In a world saturated with disposable fashion, supercheap purses and scarves you can order from an Instagram ad, Hermès's famous Birkin bags sell for more used than new.

They simply can't charge enough for their bags. In fact, the more they charge, the more people desire them. There's actually a term for this phenomenon that you might have heard in an Econ 101 class: a Veblen good—and Birkin bags are often the poster child.

But it's no gimmick. Hermès ruthlessly controls the quality of their bags—it's said it can take an entire day just to make one. They don't even consider their luxury goods to be fashion, instead describing them as *vêtements-objets*—essentially clothing as art. You don't simply buy them; you *collect* them.

(I think similarly about House of Tamworth creative grenades: You don't just drink them; you collect them, and you display them in your house.)

You want to talk about buzzy shoe drops from PUMA? Literally everything new that Hermès releases garners hype. They always control the amount of anything they release, selling their products only in official Hermès stores, which are still majority family owned after all these years.

(That's also why I'm so keen on selling Tamworth products from my own Art in the Age stores across the country.)

And yes, Hermès has brand mysticism. Of course they have brand mysticism. I mean, Hermès is named after a literal freaking god! The Greek god of messengers and commerce, to be exact. You probably didn't even know the brand began as a harness and saddle maker for horses and even today still sells high-end equestrian stuff. How cool is that?

That's another reason why, even during COVID, they remained rock-solid. It was reported that after China lifted lockdown restrictions in April 2020, Hermès pulled in $2.7 million *in one day* at its flagship store in Guangzhou.

How could a company that sells $15,000 handbags and $9,000 jumping saddles thrive during a crisis where so many people were broke, rarely leaving their homes, and literally tightening their purse strings?

Because they have the transformative enchantment of a brand world they've built over centuries.

(And, okay, it's certainly also possible that a lot of rich dicks had nothing else to spend their ballooning wealth on during the pandemic. But many other ultra-luxury brands flopped during the same time frame, so Hermès was doing something right.)

I'd like to think I'm building toward what Hermès is with Tamworth Distilling. Sometimes I think our prices are high. But I'm trying to deliver a great product. And I won't overcharge if I can't make a case for it. Of course, our spirits don't cost tens of thousands of dollars like a Birkin bag, but we still like to think they are so well made, so unique, so singular, so rare, that there's literally no replacement.

Certainly not some replacement Amazon or Uber will ever be capable of selling one day, maybe even soon.

And I think—I hope!—that by the time my grandkids are running the spirits brand, it will be as potent as Hermès.

LESSON 8

TURN YOUR BRAND INTO A CULT

Cults Transcend Borders

WHETHER YOU'RE HERMÈS or Tamworth Distilling, when you create a brand, when you launch a product, you're hoping to quickly attract the sorts of early adopters who will really understand the brand, become obsessed with it, and then begin to champion it.

This is your cult.

With Sailor Jerry, for instance, the cult was what I'd call the Scruffy Old-School Tattoo Set. We weren't talking about bro types with tribal ink or teeny-boppers with "Live Laugh Love" on their wrists.

With Hendrick's, it was sophisticated and smart, big-city drinkers on the cutting edge of craft spirits and mixology. We started calling these people Unusualists in the media. So you'd hear that term and you'd either want to be part of our tribe—"Hey, I'm unique, I'm unusual!"—or you might be scared off. That's fine too.

For Art in the Age, we had what we dubbed Overeducated Bohemian Agrarians. It's a nicer way of saying smartypants, environmentally concerned hipsters.

Most brands go as broad as possible—they'll claim their gin is for young and old, big-city and country folks, vodka and whiskey lovers, etc.—trying to create a mainstream hit by making something that everyone will like.

That's impossible.

If you try to create something that everyone will like right off the bat, all you get is bland, boring products.

At QCM, what we try to do is get a smaller group of people passionate about the brand right out of the gate. Yes, cults are built on cultural and mutual interests. But the way you build your cult is extremely nuanced and intuitive.

We purposefully make our products somewhat polarizing. Hopefully that will turn a smaller group into superfreak ambassadors for our products—and then the word will spread from there.

Then, and only then, does a brand have a chance to go mainstream. If you try to make it mainstream right out of the gate, chances are it won't have that unique element that makes it stick.

First, our goal is to always create things that we like ourselves. Because we assume we have good taste and if we like something, others will like it too. It might not be a ton of people, but a cult will form if we've been true to ourselves and designed something for a select group.

With Sailor Jerry, we had a hunch that the same kind of people that get old-school tattoos would tend to drink the same Kool-Aid. (Or high-proof spiced rum.) We were right.

With Hendrick's, we try to make things that are deliberately polarizing. Whether people either really, really love something or really, really hate something, they tend to talk about it more. That gives it a snowball's chance in hell of actually breaking out and garnering buzz.

How can you not talk about a beaver anus whiskey?

When we create brands for bigger companies, they always make us go through their intense market research process. And while we understand why they need to do this, this process tends to reduce ideas to the lowest common denominator—or flat-out kill interesting ideas altogether.

The test subjects are people desperate for $75, a complimentary doughnut, and a free can of Dr. Pepper. I don't really care if they don't like the shape of a bottle; I don't care if they don't easily understand the name of our new gin. What do they know?

The fact is, if you make something too broad, it won't become sticky.

I always say, "Middle of the road leads to roadkill."

You can also make a product too niche, of course. You see that all the time with movies and records that are so strange and experimental that it is literally impossible for more than a few thousand people to become fans of them.

The key thing you have to ask yourself when creating anything is, Who would be attracted to this?

You might not exactly know, and that can be okay. We certainly didn't when we launched The Deer Slayer. We just knew it was crazy enough, it was differentiated enough, it was divisive enough that *some* group would eventually start talking about it.

I have that same hunch about some of our upcoming launches too.

CHEKHOV'S GRENADES

SALEM WITCH WHISKEY, GOING BATSHIT CRAZY, AND THANKSGIVING IN A GLASS

IT'S FEBRUARY 2021, it's snowing outside, and I'm sitting in a meeting with our liquid development team. I'm in my upstairs home office in Philadelphia, my marketing team from Quaker City Mercantile is Zooming in, and the distillers and lab people are videoing in from New Hampshire.

"So what do we got?" I ask.

This is a pitch session, something we frequently do.

Someone says there's a certain fungus that grows on rye grains and replaces the shoots with a purple-black growth called sclerotia. It contains lysergic acid and ergotamine, which, when consumed by humans, can cause convulsions, muscle spasms, gangrene, the feeling that there's something crawling under your skin, and severe hallucinations. Lysergic acid, in fact, is the same substance from which the drug LSD is synthesized.

And guess what, he says, these are the same symptoms exhibited by some of the convicted Salem witches, who had no doubt just eaten bad rye bread in the 1600s. It's groovy with the GRAS list too; the TTB will actually allow you to use rye grain covered in this fungus. It would be distilled out, of course, so it wouldn't be dangerous. But we could still make a rye whiskey and say, "It tastes like a trip."

That's pretty good.

What else you got?

This is how you keep a team engaged, I've found. These big-group brainstorming sessions where the distillers are very much part of the discussion with the marketing team and the retail team and me and my crazy ideas—everyone gets to weigh in.

Another person says, Have you heard about these secret bat caves up here in New Hampshire?

Sure.

Well, if you didn't know, guano—bat manure—is sometimes used as a nitrate to cure meat. We could potentially use that nitrate and make a bat-guano whiskey.

We'll call it Batshit Crazy.

That's hysterical, and it would no doubt get talked about online...

But probably not in a good way. It certainly feels a little tone-deaf as we come to the end of a pandemic supposedly caused by bats.

Everyone agrees.

A distiller says, The same way you can milk a cow, you can milk a donkey. It's called ass milk. And in Mongolia, they make vodka from goat's milk. The TTB allows spirits to be made from milk but doesn't specify what kind of milk it needs to be. He suggests that we get milk from our local moose population. We could ferment it, then distill it.

True, New Hampshire has a lot of moose, but what fucking moose is going to let you milk it?

We all agree that no one here wants to milk a one-ton moose.

Fig. 35 A Glass of Gobble

Ideas are flying fast. Since we are always planning products at least a year ahead, we need lots of them.

Have you heard about the Sonoran Desert toad in Mexico? someone asks. If you lick it, it makes you hallucinate. Another person suggests that we could get a bunch of them and let them swim around in the water we use to make our whiskey.

Someone jokes that we could call it Toad Licker.

Toad Liquor.

I laugh.

I like that idea, but it really has nothing to do with New Hampshire. Sometimes an idea is good, but you have to pass on it if it doesn't fit your ethos.

It used to be that my marketing team and I would come up with all the ideas and then tell the distillers, "Figure out how to make this shit."

That wasn't the best system. Now the distillers tell me what ingredients and processes they are interested in, and then I figure out the storytelling.

Or if someone comes up with a really great name, a really great idea, the distillers immediately tell us if they can make it—if they even want to make it. They're ultimately the bosses because they can do things the rest of us can't.

What we're trying to do is create storytelling and liquid development from a holistic place, then try to marry them together.

Finally someone says that New Hampshire has a lot of turkeys. Why don't we repeat The Deer Slayer but use turkey instead?

A literal wild turkey whiskey!

That's a good troll and a great idea.

Yeah, yeah. I'm into it.

Maybe we could add cranberries and potatoes, maybe even stuffing and herbs. It would be literal Thanksgiving in a glass. Every year all these articles come out about how to "drink your Thanksgiving," and they're always silly. Some Wild Turkey with potato vodka and cranberry liqueur, and you get the drift.

Lame.

But this would truly be the first-ever Thanksgiving meal all in one bottle.

A gobbler for your gullet.

We'll call it Bird of Courage.

That's what Ben Franklin dubbed turkeys when he made the case that the turkey should be our national bird, not the bald eagle.

And so, on the morning of October 27, 2021, one month before Thanksgiving, we actually tossed that creative grenade into the world.

An explosion of virality followed.

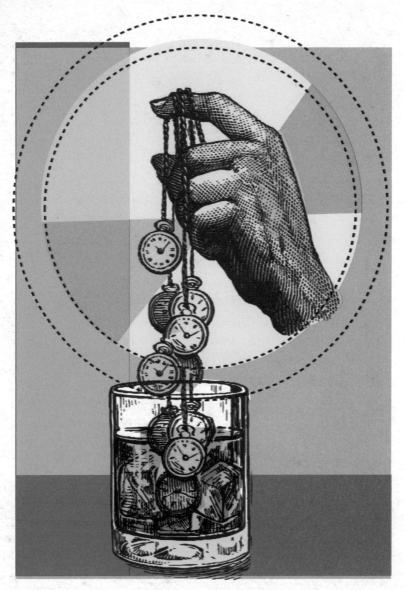

Fig. 36 You Are Getting Sleepy . . .

★ THE MAGICAL INGREDIENT ★

TIME

How to Not Fail: Don't Bet the Farm

THE DAYS OF SPENDING $30 MILLION to launch a new product are over. You can't rely on having that kind of budget anymore. And the moment the ad support is gone, everything can just collapse. Look at Prizefight, for example.

I always say it's really easy to come up with a great brand. Branding new liquid—I can do that all day long. I have a zillion good ideas in that regard.

The hard part is making it stick.

The hard part is getting anyone to notice it.

There are just so many choices out there.

Sometimes I can't believe how hard it is to break through and be heard. It can feel like dropping a pebble in the ocean and hoping it makes waves.

It takes so much time to get the momentum going. Money can speed things up, but it can't accomplish everything. I much prefer to try out lots of stuff on the cheap. I never bet the farm, as they say.

Instead of doing years of testing, as the big boys do, at QCM, we try to launch something out into the marketplace once it's "close enough for jazz," as they say. Then we pivot like hell until it takes off, riffing and continually adding "notes" to the composition.

If something isn't working, you cut your minor losses.

If you notice something *is* working, you do more of it!

Ernest Gallo, the legendary winery owner, with whom I did a cool line of vermouths called Lo-Fi Aperitifs, once told me, "When I see smoke, I'll pour gasoline on it."

What he meant was that when he noticed something was working organically, only then would he start paying to promote it. Money is a great accelerant, but before you spend your money, you have to have everything worked out; you have to have your onion formed; you have to have your brand mysticism imagined and developed.

{177}

Take the whole music component of Sailor Jerry. It happened completely by accident and then ended up being a key strategy in making the brand explode in ways that we didn't even fully comprehend until months later.

We had this store, and we sold shitty T-shirts, and we tried to promote our rum. That was what we did. Then out of the blue, we hired a real punk dude. So suddenly this guy with a huge mohawk was now stocking the clothes. One day he casually mentioned to me that he was going to bring Social Distortion, the great California punk band, by the store.

"You know Social Distortion?"

"Yeah, they're buddies of mine," he told me. "We can try to get a photo op."

I told him not to be too obvious. Make it organic. So when they came in, we just sat them on a couch in front of a coffee table with a bunch of bottles of rum and some empty glasses. They eventually picked them up, looked at them, and started drinking the Sailor Jerry—and I took their picture. We posted the photos in the store, and that was enough.

Soon, whenever a band was in town on tour, they'd come by the store. These weren't top 40 bands, but they were huge with our core cult audience.

The Buzzcocks, the Reverend Horton Heat, Stiff Little Fingers, Eagles of Death Metal, Jay Reatard.

These were the kinds of bands that still travel around in a beat-up van from town to town.

Eventually we started inviting them to play concerts on the sidewalk in front of the store. That was technically not legal in Philadelphia, but we tricked the city under a loophole: If you're filming a movie, the city will shut down the street for you. Even give you a police escort. So that was what we always said we were doing.

Fans would flood these blocked-off streets. Every band, big or small, has their own group of loyal fans, so suddenly Sailor Jerry had an entrée into each band's cult. Then we'd "pay" the band in free clothes and a case of rum—they'd drive off to the next town on their tour, espousing the greatness of Sailor Jerry Rum, sharing it across the country, and telling every other band to be sure and visit our store whenever they were in Philly.

Not only would we have the bands play the store, we'd also design flyers and posters for them. We'd set up photo shoots we paid for. We started putting out music compilation CDs featuring all the bands that had played Sailor Jerry and then gave away thousands of these CDs across the country. (Remember, this was before Spotify and even Napster.)

The music not only promoted the bands but also gave Sailor Jerry Rum its own soundtrack, adding authenticity and another layer to the onion.

In the summer of 2008, on the literal day that we sold Sailor Jerry to WGS, they had their execs in Philadelphia. And the store coincidentally had Paint It Black, a local hardcore band, playing a concert they called "Destroy the Street." There was absolutely insane energy as thousands of people moshed on the closed-off street. I think the WGS bigwigs were terrified that it was going to spin out of control, yet as they huddled safely inside the store, I saw that the suits were also insanely excited at all the energy and momentum the brand already had built into it.

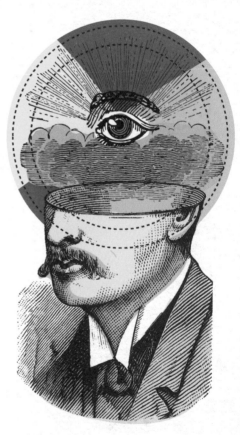

I fucking love the kind of marketing that doesn't cost a ton of money yet gets tons of buzz.

The thing is, though, you need good brand ambassadors who can follow up these kinds of stunts by getting "liquid to lips." If people have heard about your product—if people simply know they can get a free concert out of that rum brand but never have an opportunity to taste it—well, then, your marketing has ultimately failed.

Fig. 37 Open Your Mind

Recently, there was an "artisan" ice-cream brand in Brooklyn that was doing quite well. Lines around the block. They started opening more and more locations. They built a giant factory. They got a deal with Disney World. Oprah was a big fan! And they quit focusing on their ice cream.

I know I shit on Brooklyn a lot, but that's the problem with starting a brand in Brooklyn. If it starts to work and get a little attention, the Wall Street money douches arrive, and then the celebrities. You start believing the hype, and you quit working out your fundamentals of growth; you quit working on a timeline you can handle. It would be as if we just let Taylor Swift play in front of the Sailor Jerry store in 2008 because she was famous and Universal Music Group wanted her to.

It simply wouldn't fit within the brand's mythology.

Currently, with Tamworth Distilling, we are selling out of everything we make, we are bursting at the seams, but we're continuing to grow slowly, at our own pace. To grow fast would mean we'd need to take on millions of dollars in investment. We don't want to do that. We don't want investors to dictate our growth.

But I do believe there is a larger market out there for Tamworth Distilling, that there is smoke worth pouring gasoline on.

That is why, in the summer of 2021, we purchased another 105 acres of land. Soon we'll be able to have more barrel houses, additional stills, and room for a lot more farming. We are also going to start composting and selling our waste. We're likewise moving toward more sustainable energy, mostly solar.

It's all part of a carefully considered thirty-year growth plan.

I'm giddy at the thought of what Tamworth Distilling might look like by 2050.

It's fun to imagine what we will be producing then, what the spirits industry will even look like by then, and how we will still be finding ways to grab your attention.

THE FINAL LESSON
CONTINUALLY FIND WAYS TO GENERATE BUZZ AND BLOW PEOPLE'S FUCKING MINDS

THAT'S WHY THE CURIOSITY, the creativity can never stop. You can't just rest on your past successes.

After having read this book, I hope you see that everything I do, even creative grenades—especially creative grenades—is created through storytelling. That inspiration comes from getting offline and exploring things from the past.

So does my latest idea.

I've been obsessed with France lately, and I recently read Andrew Roberts's 790-page *Napoleon: A Life*. Did you know the diminutive emperor ordered fifty bottles of cologne a month from his perfumer? He was obsessed with scent, and the book in turn detailed the French perfume making of his era along with the early days of alchemy.

It really got me thinking about how we might take Tamworth to the next level . . .

. . . and generate the most buzz we ever have.

I wondered, Could we make a drinkable "perfume"?

Of course, not everyone wants to drink a deer-blood whiskey or whatever. Might ladies want some rose-petal spirit they could drink *and* spray behind their ears?

Would this fill a void?

Maybe.

My wife even found a perfumer who makes an edible perfume that you can spray on food. It's apparently pretty bitter.

I started thinking along the lines of a spirit that is just incredibly aromatic. Like the most aromatic spirit ever made.

So I went to Matt and Jamie and asked them how we could capture the essence of ingredients the same way they do with perfumes. I told them I really want to get spirits back to the essence of what they initially were: a distillation of these wonderful living things.

Fig. 38 I Wonder What This Button Does?

But they didn't get it. This happens sometimes.

At first, they both really struggled to wrap their heads around the whole idea. "Aren't perfumes denatured and inherently undrinkable?" they asked me.

That's true. If you actually drank the perfume on your vanity, it would taste like poison.

So I tried to explain that I don't want a literal perfume. Although it occurs to me . . . maybe we *should* include an atomizer with the packaging so you can spray it on . . . your drinks.

Suddenly I find myself back where I started in the booze business—with gin. With Hendrick's.

Everything comes full circle.

Ingredient-wise, I think gin is one of the few spirits where you can really be close to the origins of the word "spirits"—what alchemists call the transmutation of the life force of botanicals into a different form.

With gin, you're really close to turning fresh ingredients into something utterly exquisite.

Of course, this drinkable perfume would have to be super high-proof. That's the only way to fully extract things such as rose petals and other essences. This is how my mind is working. If it's high-proof, maybe it should come in the same 200-mL bottles that our House of Tamworth experiments come in.

These could be part of our Tamworth Garden series. An experimental extension of our gin line. I want to see how far it can go. How much closer can this get me to my own bottle of Hermès? Could we charge $100 for 200 mL? Could we charge $1,000?

Then it would really have to feel like it's worth it.

The most extraordinary gin the world has ever seen.

As I'm in the final edits of this book, Matt is in the lab with rotovaps and all sorts of newfangled equipment I don't fully understand. He builds spirits like this from a molecular level. It's the summer, and he's mastering new ways to take that life force of botanicals and inject it into this gin in a very fresh way to make a perfume you can drink.

He's finally figured it out.

And as I watch him work, the analogy hits me.

Our minds are just like a gin.

A gin starts as a grain-neutral spirit. A blank slate. It's boring and uninteresting. You then load it up with the expected botanicals. Juniper and citrus. Then more interesting and enchanting ones. Saffron and anise. New ideas and ones from the past. Some might not even seem complementary, such as cassia and cardamom, but that's why they're perfect together, creating something greater than the sum of their parts. Creating an onion.

You likewise fill your empty mind with all these ideas, all these inspirations over the years, all these arcane thoughts from the past that everyone else has already forgotten, and then you finally distill it into one grand vision. One great idea. Or a work of art. Or a great brand. Or a book.

The distillation of your own life force.

Right as this book is going to print, Tamworth Garden SEACOAST ROSE Perfume of Gin will be going through the stills.

And as this book is being bound and packaged, it will be getting bottled and labeled.

This book will ship to bookstores and warehouses around the country, and SEA-COAST ROSE Perfume of Gin will be put on our own shelves in New Hampshire and Philadelphia.

You'll buy this book, and maybe you'll buy the gin too.

And hopefully both will fill your mind with enjoyment and thought, inspiring you to cultivate your own curiosity, to find those new ideas and add them to your brain like botanicals, which you will then distill into your own great products, brands, companies, and works of art in this world.

I really hope you do. I can't wait to drink them up.

Thank-Yous

STEVEN GRASSE: I'd like to thank my senior staff, who, for some reason, have stuck with me through thick and thin over the past three decades. Especially Rona, Jerry, Ron P., Ron S., Joe, Kate, Alison, Sarah, and Dave S. (You guys must be gluttons for punishment!)

I'd like to thank my many clients for sharing and prospering from our unique vision. In particular the Grant family . . . what a long, strange trip it's been.

I'd like to thank my wife, Sonia, for being an amazing creative and life partner. You have opened my mind to new worlds of enchantment and wonder.

I'd like to thank my mom and dad for teaching me how to be creative and how to work hard and get shit done. And my brother Dave for his help in realizing our vision in the middle of nowhere New Hampshire.

I'd like to thank Aaron for helping me to articulate all this mumbo jumbo. And Clare, my agent, for finding a publisher crazy enough to buy it. And Running Press for being that crazy publisher.

Pretty much everyone else can fuck off. Especially my high school guidance counselor, who told me that people like me don't amount to much and I'd be lucky to get into community college.

AARON GOLDFARB: Thank you to Steve for giving me the single most compelling, enthralling, and hilarious interview I've ever conducted back in 2018—it would ultimately lay the foundation for our friendship and this book. To Clare Pelino for bringing us together professionally to get this thing done. And thanks to my wife and children, who rarely read anything I write but may turn to this page to see if they are mentioned—I so appreciate the support.

STEVEN GRASSE is the founder of Quaker City Mercantile and the creator of Hendrick's Gin, Sailor Jerry Rum, Art in the Age Spirits, and Tamworth Distilling, among many others. He has also helped revive legacy brands such as Narragansett, Miller High Life, Guinness, and Pilsner Urquell. He has written the books *The Evil Empire: 101 Ways That England Ruined the World*, *Colonial Spirits: A Toast to Our Drunken History*, and *The Cocktail Workshop: An Essential Guide to Classic Drinks and How to Make Them Your Own*. He lives in Philadelphia and New Hampshire with his family.

Aaron Goldfarb is a novelist, author, and journalist who frequently writes about the spirits industry and drinking culture for the *New York Times*, *Esquire*, *PUNCH*, and *VinePair*. His two most recent books are *Hacking Whiskey: Smoking, Blending, Fat-Washing, and Other Whiskey Experiments* and *Gather Around Cocktails: Drinks to Celebrate Usual and Unusual Holidays*. His 2018 *VinePair* article on Grasse, "How Do You Make a Booze Brand Go Viral?," fittingly went viral itself and has since been shared online hundreds of thousands of times. He was named 2020's Best Cocktail and Spirits Writer at Tales of the Cocktail's Spirited Awards. He lives in Brooklyn with his family.